Democratic Schools

DEMOCRATIC
SCHOOLS

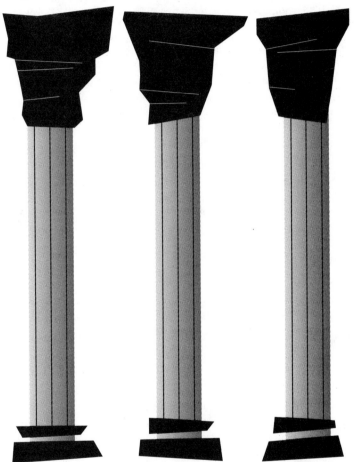

EDITED BY MICHAEL W. APPLE AND JAMES A. BEANE

ASCD

ASSOCIATION FOR SUPERVISION AND CURRICULUM DEVELOPMENT
ALEXANDRIA, VIRGINIA

Association for Supervision and Curriculum Development
1250 N. Pitt Street, Alexandria, VA 22314
Telephone (703) 549-9110, Fax (703) 549-3891

Printed in the United States of America.

Gene R. Carter, *Executive Director*
Ronald S. Brandt, *Executive Editor*
Nancy Modrak, *Managing Editor, ASCD Books*
Julie Houtz, *Senior Associate Editor*
Gary Bloom, *Manager, Design and Production Services*
Karen Monaco, *Senior Graphic Designer*
Stephanie Justen, *Production Coordinator*
Valerie Sprague, *Desktop Publisher*

ASCD Stock No.: 1-95052
$14.95

From the Editors: We welcome readers' comments on ASCD books and other publications. If you would like to give us your opinion of this book or suggest topics for future books, please write to ASCD, Managing Editor of Books, 1250 N. Pitt St., Alexandria, VA 22314.

Library of Congress Cataloging-in-Publication Data

Democratic schools / edited by Michael W. Apple and James A. Beane.
     p.   cm.
    Includes bibliographical references (p.).
    ISBN 0-87120-241-7
    1. Public schools—United States—Case studies.   2. Democracy—
  Study and teaching—United States—Case studies.   3. Critical
  pedagogy—United States—Case studies.   4. Educational equalization—
  United States—Case studies.   I. Apple, Michael W.   II. Beane,
  James A., 1994–   .
    LA217.2.D45   1995
    370.11'5—dc20
                                95-7784
                                CIP

Foreword

Upon reviewing a copy of the manuscript for this book, I searched on a high shelf in my office library for a book that I have not read in several years, John Dewey's classic *Democracy and Education* (New York: Macmillan, 1916). After locating the book, I turned to the chapter called "The Democratic Conception in Education." In it, Dewey says that a democratic society "must have a type of education which gives individuals a personal interest in social relationships and control, and the habits of mind which secure social change without introducing disorder" (p. 115).

"The ideal," Dewey says, "may seem remote of execution, but the democratic ideal of education is a farcical yet tragic delusion except as the ideal more and more dominates our public system of education" (p. 114).

The authors of *Democratic Schools* share Dewey's belief that the democratic ideal of education must pervade the public schools, and the schools they describe reinforce the wisdom of striving for "the ideal." These schools offer students the very qualities that Dewey says should characterize education in a democratic society: shared interests, freedom in interaction, participation, and social relationships.

The educators in these schools are described as people who both value and practice the democratic way of life. As editors Michael Apple and James Beane emphasize, democratic schools cannot exist without the leadership of educators who provide students with learning experiences that promote the democratic way of life. While acknowledging that in most schools the gap between democratic values and school practices is as wide now as ever, the editors convincingly argue that the schools featured in this book are evidence of the power of democratic practices in an education setting. That these schools are public schools is especially reassuring, they say, because privatization of the public schools is being widely discussed and promoted. The editors deliberately chose stories of public schools for this book because they believe that democratic school reforms can be a powerful and positive force for the revitalization of public schools.

The writers of this book do not allow the confusion surrounding the meaning of democracy to deter them from the task of convincing people of the urgent need for democratic schools. I hope *Democratic Schools* moves you to assess your own school, to think about whether your school could rightly be called a democratic school. And I hope those of you who *are* working in democratic schools will respond to the editors' request to write about your own experiences, for I look forward to reading more stories about public schools that work, as Apple and Beane say, "by bringing real democracy to life."

— CHARLES PATTERSON
ASCD President, 1995–96

1

The Case for Democratic Schools

JAMES A. BEANE AND MICHAEL W. APPLE

Pasadena, CA, 1937. *A group of 3rd graders has spent several weeks studying problems in their school, homes, neighborhoods, and community. Besides looking at problems they know of, they have also gathered examples from parents, teachers, and community officials. After a month of research and discussion, they collect their recommendations for solving these problems in a booklet that will be distributed throughout the community.*

Baltimore, MD, 1953. *The streets in one neighborhood of this city are filled for a week by high school students conducting a door-to-door voter registration drive among ethnic minority residents. This is but one of many projects they have worked on this year, including a civil defense survey, a community health campaign, and a study of housing relocation problems.*

Port Jarvis, NY, 1972. *Though it is a cold, snowy night, nearly 125 students, teachers, administrators, parents, board members, and representatives of various community organizations are meeting to consider projects they might undertake to redesign their schools. Among others, they will make arrangements to distribute school newsletters in languages other than English, plan a new community youth center, start a radio program produced by students, set up mentorships for young*

1

people with adults in the community, and arrange to make the school more available for community activities.

Ulysses, PA, 1979. *Just as they do every Friday afternoon, the students and teachers in the elementary school gather today to discuss ongoing schoolwide projects and problems. The major issue this week is that someone has written graffiti on a school wall. After nearly a half-hour of debate, three proposals are put forth. The group votes to establish a new rule: anyone defacing school property will spend their free time over three days working with the school custodian.*

Belvidere, IL, 1990. *Looking out a classroom window at the dumpster below, a student asks the teacher, "Where does that garbage go?" Just as curious, the teacher arranges for a class field trip to an area landfill. Concerned about the size and contents of the landfill, the students undertake a campaign for conservation and recycling in their school. Over several months, their efforts begin to take hold. Though they are just 1st graders, they have made a difference in their school.*

Madison, WI, 1991. *On a warm September day, a group of nearly 60 middle school students and their teachers are working together to create their curriculum out of questions and concerns they have about them-selves and their world. Eventually they cluster their questions into themes like "Living in the Future," "Problems in the Environment," "Isms," and "Conflict." After selecting their first theme and planning relevant activities, they will spend the year trying to answer those questions—their questions.*

All of us have heard stories like these and know that while not rare, they are unusual. All took place in public schools. All involved real young people, real educators, and real communities no different on the surface than thousands of others. Yet there is something about these stories, a sometimes elusive feeling, that appeals to a deep sense of what a worthwhile and valuable education ought to look like. What are these people working on? Who is involved? How are they working together? Who benefits from such work? If we think about these stories and questions, we may eventually begin to see what is really happening. And perhaps we will begin to remember a now half-forgotten idea that was to guide the purposes and programs of our public schools. The idea was, and is, democracy.

In the midst of widespread attacks on education, we must keep alive the long tradition of democratic school reform that has played such a valuable role in making many schools lively and powerful places for those who go to them. Rather than giving up on the idea of the "public" schools and moving down the path toward privatization, we need to focus on schools that work. Despite some people's relentless attempts to make us think otherwise, we do not have to resign ourselves to choosing between a failing public school system and market initiatives such as voucher plans or for-profit "public" schools run by private firms like the Edison Project or Education Alternatives Inc. There are public schools throughout this country where the hard work of teachers, administrators, parents, community activists, and students has paid off. These are the schools that are alive with excitement, even in sometimes depressing and difficult circumstances. These are the schools in which teachers and students alike are engaged in serious work that results in rich and vital learning experiences for all.

The idea of democratic schools has fallen on hard times, however. All around us, we can see the signs. Public schools are called on to educate all of our children, yet are simultaneously blamed for the social and economic disparities that severely detract from their chances of successfully doing so. Local decision making is glorified in political rhetoric at the same time that legislation is introduced to put in place national standards, a national curriculum, and national tests. Demands are made to emphasize critical thinking while censorship of school programs and materials increases. Census figures display growing cultural diversity while pressure is applied to keep the curriculum within the narrow boundaries of the Western cultural tradition. The needs of business and industry are suddenly the preeminent goals of our educational system. Education in morality and ethics is reduced to a litany of behavior traits. Privileged groups seek to flee comprehensive, diverse public schools through vouchers, tax credits, "choice" plans, and exclusionary programs for their "gifted" children. Federal officials pronounce the public schools a failure while effectively suppressing a report that shows these officials have misused their own statistics (Jensen 1994).

Could it be that the century-long struggle for democratic purposes and practices in education and schooling never occurred? How could our collective memory have failed so easily? *Thematic unit teaching* and *curriculum integration* have become buzz words in educational circles, but have we forgotten that both concepts have their roots in the problem-centered "core" approaches advocated by earlier progressive social reconstructionists? How can we disconnect the call for heterogeneous grouping, advocated by so many groups today, from the longer struggle of the civil rights movement? Are "developmentally appropriate" practices a recent invention, or do they stretch back to the progressive, child-centered schools created early in this century? When we speak of cooperative learning today, shall we simply ignore the cooperative group process work done in schools and communities as part of democratic movements since the 1920s? How can we seem puzzled by ways to connect schools to their communities when so many stories of significant service projects can be found in the professional literature of at least the past sixty years?

Rosa Parks is often portrayed during Black History Month as simply a "tired, older woman" who wanted to sit down on a bus. But her courageous act on that bus came after months of work on resistance and civil disobedience at the Highlander Folk School. Likewise, many of our most trusted and powerful ideas about schooling are the hard-won gains of long and courageous efforts to make our schools more democratic (see, for example, Rugg 1939). We are the beneficiaries of those efforts, and we have an obligation to carry forward the demanding dream of public schools for a democratic society.

The questions raised here are meant to remind us of that half-forgotten dream, to rouse us from the stupor we fell into nearly twenty years ago. Although our memories may have become blurred, we can still recall that public schools are essential to democracy. We cannot help but be jolted wide awake when discussions about what works in schools, what should be done in schools, make no mention of the role of public schools in expanding the democratic way of life. And so we must make the case again.

The Meaning of Democracy

Those of us who live in the United States claim that democracy is the central tenet of our social and political relations. It is, we say, the basis for how we govern ourselves, the concept by which we measure the wisdom and worth of social policies and shifts, the ethical anchor we seek when our political ship seems to drift. And it is the standard we use to measure the political progress of other countries as well as their trade status with our own.

It is not surprising, then, that the word "democracy," seems to be heard more frequently these days. In many places around the world, oppressed peoples struggle for human and civil rights. Dictatorships and popularly elected governments are overthrown at a startling rate. In the United States, growing numbers of people claim that politicians at all levels are no longer in touch with their constituents. Conflict among political, religious, and cultural groups fuels debate over free speech, privacy, land use, lifestyles, and, throughout it all, the rights of the individual in relation to the interests of the larger society. Amid this dissonance, the idea of democracy presumably serves as a crucial benchmark for judging events and ideas.

Central tenets and ethical anchors, however, also tend to be converted into rhetorical slogans and political codes to gain popular support for all manner of ideas. Thus, they are fraught with ambiguity. "Democracy" is no exception. Woodrow Wilson understood this well when he deflected opposition to U.S. involvement in World War I with the virtually unassailable statement that our soldiers were fighting "to make the world safe for democracy." Calling forth the word "democracy" did the trick then and has done so for a wide array of political and military maneuvers since.

The meaning of democracy is just as ambiguous in our own times, and the rhetorical convenience of that ambiguity is more evident than ever (Apple 1988). One can understand, for example, how claims for democracy could be used to shore up movements for civil rights, expanded voting privileges, and protection of free speech. Democracy is also used, however, to further the causes of free market economies and school-choice vouchers, and to defend the dominance of two major political parties. We hear the democracy defense used countless times everyday to justify almost anything people want to do: "Hey, we live in a democracy, right?"

On the other hand, it is not uncommon to hear some people say that democracy has simply become irrelevant, that it is too inefficient or dangerous in an increasingly complex world. For these people, the democracy defense itself has become cumbersome or, perhaps, not sufficient to get them what they want. In the United States, where there are clear divisions of wealth and power, the freedoms and ambiguity associated with democracy have clearly benefited some people more than others. Efforts to sharpen the definition of democracy and extend its meaning throughout society are seen by some of the more privileged people of this country as threats to their own status and power. To understand this view, we need only look at the startling contradiction between the movement for greater school achievement on the one hand and the resistance to equitable spending for all schools on the other.

Under these complicated conditions, a book on democratic schools may seem almost foolhardy. After all, if the meaning of democracy is so confused in the larger society, how can we possibly settle on its meaning for everyday life in schools? That risk in mind, we have gone ahead, buoyed by certain beliefs. We believe that democracy does mean something and that bringing that meaning to light is critical at a time when many citizens are vigorously debating the future course of our schools. Moreover, we find it hard to imagine that people who have known the privileges of democracy would so easily give them up. We find it even harder to imagine that they would not want these privileges for their children, indeed for all people. We admit to having what Dewey and others have called the "democratic faith," the fundamental belief that democracy has a powerful meaning, that it can work, and that it is necessary if we are to maintain freedom and human dignity in our social affairs.

Democracy works in multiple ways in social affairs. Most of us who attended school in the United States (and perhaps elsewhere) were taught that democracy is a form of political governance involving the consent of the governed and equality of opportunity. For example, we learned that citizens may directly and fully participate in such events as elections while being represented in other matters by those we elect to federal and state legislatures as well as boards and committees governing local school policy.

Less explicitly taught were the conditions on which a democracy depends, the foundations of "the democratic way of life" (Beane 1990). It is these conditions and their extension through education that are the central concerns of democratic schools. Among such conditions are the following:

1. The open flow of ideas, regardless of their popularity, that enables people to be as fully informed as possible.

2. Faith in the individual and collective capacity of people to create possibilities for resolving problems.

3. The use of critical reflection and analysis to evaluate ideas, problems, and policies.

4. Concern for the welfare of others and "the common good."

5. Concern for the dignity and rights of individuals and minorities.

6. An understanding that democracy is not so much an "ideal" to be pursued as an "idealized" set of values that we must live and that must guide our life as a people.

7. The organization of social institutions to promote and extend the democratic way of life.

If people are to secure and maintain a democratic way of life, they must have opportunities to learn what that way of life means and how it might be led (Dewey 1916). Although common sense alone tells us this is a true statement, there is perhaps no more problematic concept in education than that of democratic schools, a concept that some consider almost an oxymoron. How can this be so? Simply put, many people believe that democracy is nothing more than a form of federal government and thus does not apply to schools and other social institutions. Many also believe that democracy is a right of adults, not of young people. And some believe that democracy simply cannot work in schools.

Others are committed to the idea that the democratic way of life is built upon opportunities to learn what it is about and how to lead it. They believe that the schools, as a common experience of virtually all young people, have a moral obligation to introduce them to the democratic way of life. They know, as well, that such a life is learned by experience. It is not a status to be attained only after other things are learned. Moreover, they believe that democracy extends to all people, including the young. Finally, they believe that democracy is neither cumbersome nor dangerous, that it can work in societies and it can work in schools. As Maxine Greene (1985, p. 4) writes, "Surely it is an obligation of education in a democracy to empower the young to become members of the public, to participate, and play articulate roles in the public space."

But those committed to creating democratic schools also understand that doing so involves more than the education of the young. Democratic schools are meant to be democratic places, so the idea of democracy also extends to the many roles that adults play in the schools. This means that professional educators as well as parents, community activists, and other citizens have a right to fully informed and critical participation in creating school policies and programs for themselves and young people.

Proponents of democratic schools also realize, sometimes painfully, that exercising democracy involves tensions and contradictions. Democratic participation in decision making, for example, opens the way for antidemocratic ideas such as the continuing demands for censorship of materials, the use of public tax vouchers for private school tuition, and the maintenance of historical inequities in school life. Furthermore, there always looms the possibility of the illusion of democracy, in which authorities may invite participation so as to "engineer consent" for predetermined decisions (Graebner 1988). Such contradictions and tensions point to the fact that bringing democracy to life is always a struggle. But beyond them lies the possibility for professional educators and citizens to work together in creating more democratic schools that serve the common good of the whole community.

This book is for and about educators who are committed to democracy, who value the democratic way of life, who believe that schools can be democratic places, and who have the courage to carry those beliefs into action. In several chapters we will hear some of these educators describe, in their own voices, how they have brought the idea of democracy to life in their schools and classrooms. These are remarkable stories inasmuch as the very idea of democratic schools has proved to be so elusive to the educational community. The stories are not filled with the easy promises and slick slogans of packaged programs or systems. Instead, like almost all school stories, they reveal the hard work and commitment of real educators struggling to create and maintain arrangements that reveal the deeply held values that they, and we, believe must be acted on now. The authors of this book are fundamentally dissatisfied with the conservative solutions usually put at center stage over the past decade: tighter centralized control, standardization of content, more reductive testing, and so on. All of us believe that we must move beyond handwringing and find real answers to the question "What works in schools?"

What Is a Democratic School?

Before presenting the real-life stories in this book, we want to offer a context for their telling. What is a democratic school? What might we expect to see if we visited one? What are its underlying principles? How has the concept of democratic schools emerged over time? What threatens the existence of these schools? How can it be that these stories are so remarkable in a society that purports to be democratic?

Democratic schools, like democracy itself, do not happen by chance. They result from explicit attempts by educators to put in place arrangements and opportunities that will bring democracy to life (see, for example, Bastian et al. 1986; Wood 1988, 1992). These arrangements and opportunities involve two lines of work. One is to create democratic structures and processes by which life in the school is carried out. The other is to create a curriculum that will give young people democratic experiences.

Democratic Structures and Processes

To say that democracy rests on the consent of the governed is almost a cliché, but in a democratic school it is true that all of those directly involved in the school, including young people, have the right to participate in the process of decision making. For this reason, democratic schools are marked by widespread participation in issues of governance and policy making. Committees, councils, and other schoolwide decision-making groups include not only professional educators, but also young people, their parents, and other members of the school community. In classrooms, young people and teachers engage in collaborative planning, reaching decisions that respond to the concerns, aspirations, and interests of both. This kind of democratic planning, at both the school and the classroom levels, is not the "engineering of consent" toward predetermined decisions that has too often created the illusion of democracy, but a genuine attempt to honor the right of people to participate in making decisions that affect their lives.

We must remember, however, that local decision making must still be guided by democratic values. It is one of the contradictions of democracy that local, populist politics do not always serve democratic ends. After all, left entirely to local discretion, we might still have schools characterized by legal racial segregation and denial of access to all but the wealthy. In short, the realization of democratic schools does in part depend on selective intervention of the state, especially where the process and content of local decision making serve to disenfranchise and oppress selected groups of people. While such intervention is usually unpopular among those who have sought exclusive power, it serves as a reminder that the wide distribution of rights and other democratic values are meant to be more than principles on paper.

Our own times offer many illustrations of the tension between the state's obligation to safeguard democracy and the democratic right of interest groups to air their views. For example, public schools in a democratic society are meant to offer access to, and critical examination of, a wide range of ideas. Meanwhile, various special interest groups, especially religious fundamentalists, demand that ideas and materials open to consideration in schools be limited to those supporting their groups' own values (Delfattore 1993). At the same time, local groups across the political spectrum are troubled by moves to create a national curriculum in which the range of knowledge studied is limited to that deemed important by select groups at the national level. The idea of widespread participation in school affairs as a feature of democratic schools is thus not as simple as inviting participation, because the right to "have a say" introduces questions about how various viewpoints fit into the fragile equation balancing special interests and the larger "common good" of the democratic community.

Those involved in democratic schools see themselves as participants in communities of learning. By their very nature, these communities are diverse, and that diversity is prized, not viewed as a problem. Such communities include people who reflect differences in age, culture, ethnicity, gender, socioeconomic class, aspirations, and abilities. These differences enrich the community and the range of views it might consider. Separating people of any age on the basis of these differences or using labels to stereotype them simply creates divisions and status systems that detract from the democratic nature of the community and the dignity of the individuals against whom such practices work so harshly.

While the community prizes diversity, it also has a sense of shared purpose. No matter what the privatizers or those who want economic rationality to drive schools say, democracy is not simply a theory of self-interest that gives people license to pursue their own goals at the expense of others; the common good is a central feature of democracy. For this reason, the communities of learners in democratic schools are marked by an emphasis on cooperation and collaboration rather than competition. People see their stake in others, and arrangements are created that encourage young people to improve the life of the community by helping others.

In all these arrangements, and in the policy decisions that support them, people in democratic schools persistently emphasize structural equity. While initial access to educational opportunities is understood to be a necessary aspect of democratic schools, access alone is not considered sufficient for their realization. In an authentically democratic community, all young people are also considered to have the right of access to all programs in the school and to the outcomes the school values. For this reason, those in democratic schools seek to assure that the school includes no institutional barriers to young people. Every effort is made to eliminate tracking, biased testing, and other arrangements that so often deny such access on grounds of race, gender, and socioeconomic class.

Educators who are committed to democracy realize that sources of inequity in the school are likely to be found in the community as well. At the very least, they understand that the possibilities arising from democratic experiences in the school may too easily be washed away by life on the outside (Gutmann 1987). In seeing themselves as part of the larger community, they seek to extend democracy there, not only for the young but for all people. In short, they want democracy on a large scale; the school is just one of the sites on which they focus. This is a crucial point. The educational landscape is littered with the remains of failed school reforms, many of which failed because of the social conditions surrounding the schools. Only those reforms that recognize these conditions and actively engage them are likely to make a lasting difference in the lives of the children, educators, and communities served by the schools.

It is this last point in particular that distinguishes democratic schools from other kinds of "progressive" schools, such as those that are simply humanistic or child-centered. Democratic schools are both of those in many ways, but their vision extends beyond purposes such as improving the school climate or enhancing students' self-esteem. Democratic educators seek not simply to lessen the harshness of social inequities in school, but to change the conditions that create them. For this reason, they tie their understanding of undemocratic practices inside the school to larger conditions on the outside. The case for heterogeneous grouping, for example, is made partly on grounds of increased academic and social achievement, but more broadly on grounds of justice and equitable access as profound social issues (Oakes 1985). Like other progressive educators, those involved with democracy care deeply about young people, but they also understand that such caring requires them to stand firm against racism, injustice, centralized power, poverty, and other gross inequities in school and society.

The initial sketch of the structures and processes essential to democratic schools can be done rather quickly, but the fully rendered picture is not so easily realized. The work involved in organizing and keeping alive a democratic school is exhausting and ripe with conflict. After all, despite the rhetoric of democracy in our society and the commonsense idea that the democratic way of life is learned through democratic experiences, schools have been remarkably undemocratic institutions. While democracy emphasizes cooperation among people, too many schools have fostered competition—for grades, for status, for resources, for programs, and so on. While democracy depends upon caring for the common good, too many schools, stimulated by the influence of political agendas imposed from outside, have emphasized an idea of individuality based almost entirely on self-interest. While democracy prizes diversity, too many schools have largely reflected the interests and aspirations of the most powerful groups in this country and ignored those of the less powerful. While schools in a democracy would presumably demonstrate how to achieve equal opportunity for all, too many schools are plagued by structures like tracking and ability grouping that deny equal opportunity and results to many, particularly the poor, people of color, and women.

Those who are committed to democratic education are often placed in a position of conflict with the dominant traditions of schooling. At almost every turn, their ideas and efforts are likely to be resisted by both those who benefit from the inequities of schools and those who are more interested in efficiency and hierarchical power than in the difficult work of transforming schools from the bottom up. The frustrations involved in creating democratic schools are exceeded only by the more ambitious task of maintaining them in the face of nondemocratic currents in public opinion and educational policy. But democratic educators understand that democracy does not present an "ideal state" crisply defined and waiting to be attained. Rather, a more democratic experience is built through their continual efforts at making a difference. The undertaking is not an easy one; it is filled with contradictions, conflict, and controversy. As the old saying goes, "It was ten miles into the woods and it's ten miles out."

A Democratic Curriculum

The structures and processes discussed so far generally define the quality of everyday life in schools. As part of the longstanding traditions and deep structures of the school, they also offer powerful teachings about what and whom the school values. For this reason, they constitute a kind of "hidden" curriculum by which people learn significant lessons about justice, power, dignity, and self-worth. Democratizing these structures and processes is a crucial aspect of the schools portrayed here, but a more complete version also includes creative work toward bringing democracy to the planned or overt curriculum.

Since democracy involves the informed consent of people, a democratic curriculum emphasizes access to a wide range of information and the right of those of varied opinion to have their viewpoints heard. Educators in a democratic society have an obligation to help young people seek out a range of ideas and to voice their own. Unfortunately, many schools persistently shirk this obligation in several ways. First, they narrow the range of school-sponsored knowledge to what we might call "official" or high-status knowledge that is produced or endorsed by the dominant culture (Apple 1993). Second, they silence the voices of those outside the dominant culture, particularly people of color, women, and, of course, the young. This observation can be substantiated with little more than a glance at textbooks, reading lists, and curriculum guides.

What's most disturbing is that all too many schools have taught this official, high-status knowledge as though it were "truth" arisen from some immutable, infallible source. Those committed to a more participatory curriculum understand that knowledge is socially constructed, that it is produced and disseminated by people who have particular values, interests, and biases. This is simply a fact of life, since all of us are formed by our cultures, genders, geographies, and so on. In a democratic curriculum, however, young people learn to be "critical readers" of their society. When confronted with some knowledge or viewpoint, they are encouraged to ask questions like these: Who said this? Why did they say it? Why should we believe this? and Who benefits if we believe this and act upon it?

To clarify this point, consider an example from a classroom observed by one of this book's editors. The teacher and students were engaged in a discussion of "current events," using material from newspapers and focusing on "natural disasters." How we think about natural disasters and whose definition of what they are is crucial. For instance, we are now (unfortunately) quite used to seeing pictures of disasters in which thousands of people lose their lives to storms, drought, and so on. Like the children in that classroom, we are told to think of them as "natural" disasters. But is this seemingly neutral way of understanding current events really neutral, or are particular values smuggled in or omitted in subtle ways?

Part of the discussion that went on in that classroom provides a powerful reminder of why such a question is important. The students noted the massive mud slides that had recently occurred in South America; large numbers of people were killed or badly injured as torrential rains washed their houses down the mountainsides. Yet a closer examination reveals that little about this disaster was natural. Every year in South America there are rains, and every year people die. This particular year, an entire side of the mountain gave way; the thousands of people living on it lost their lives. No one in the valleys—the safe and fertile land—died.

Poor families are forced to live on the dangerous hillsides because this is the only land left on which they can afford to eke out a meager existence. People crowd onto the mountainsides because of poverty and historical land ownership patterns that are grossly unequal. Hence, the problem is not the yearly rain—a natural occurrence—but the unequal economic structures that allow a small minority of individuals to control the very lives of the majority of people in that region.

This altered and more complete understanding of the problem is rich in pedagogic and curricular possibilities. Helping students to understand the different ways this event could be interpreted, and the benefits to different groups of people each interpretation brings, could ultimately lead them to a richer and more ethically committed sensitivity to the societies around them (Apple 1990).

A mathematics class in an urban school provides another example of how questions are used in a democratic classroom. Students in this class were regularly given a word problem involving the cost of a monthly bus pass. They were asked to calculate whether it was cheaper to buy a monthly pass or to pay each time one went to and from work. In this particular instance, given the number of workdays that the problem writer specified, the correct answer was to pay each time. Yet built into this problem is a set of assumptions that have little bearing on the realities of these young people's lives or those of their parents.

The students knew this answer was simply wrong. After all, many of their parents worked two part-time jobs to support themselves and their families. These jobs were often at fast-food restaurants and were the only jobs available in that community after the factories had moved to take advantage of lower wages and tax breaks in other parts of the world. Thus, in the experience of these children, a person used the bus at least four times a day to get to and from work, work that was without benefits, was low paid, and was often dead-end.

This curriculum was obviously more than a little biased and insensitive. But the teacher creatively used the bias, asking students to reflect on what was wrong with this example and to think about how mathematics helped them understand their own and their parents' daily lives. In essence, she asked them to answer a question similar to those we asked above: *From whose perspective are we seeing the world in this material?* (Ladson-Billings in press). By weaving this question into the entire mathematics unit, she integrated mathematics into students' everyday lives, thus giving their work more of an impact than was ever possible in the supposedly neutral standard curriculum that was connected to the supposedly neutral standardized achievement tests that determined those young persons' futures.

At the very least, each of these examples points to the fact that someone's tradition, someone's construction of what is important to know and how it should be used, is always incorporated into our planned curriculum, often in hidden ways. As in the example of the mathematics class, however, a democratic curriculum seeks to move beyond the "selective tradition" of knowledge and meanings endorsed by the dominant culture, toward a wider range of views and voices (Williams 1961, Apple 1990). In a democratic society, no one individual or interest group can claim sole ownership of possible knowledge and meaning. Likewise, a democratic curriculum includes not only what adults think is important, but also the questions and concerns that young people have about themselves and their world. A democratic curriculum invites young people to shed the passive role of knowledge consumers and assume the active role of "meaning makers." It recognizes that people acquire knowledge by both studying external sources and engaging in complex activities that require them to construct their own knowledge.

As we have previously seen, the democratic way of life engages the creative process of seeking ways to extend and expand the values of democracy. This process, however, is not simply a participatory conversation about just anything. Rather, it is directed toward intelligent and reflective consideration of problems, events, and issues that arise in the course of our collective lives. A democratic curriculum involves continuous opportunities to explore such issues, to imagine responses to problems, and to act upon those responses. For example, the curriculum includes learning experiences organized around problems and issues such as "Conflict," "The Future of Our Community," "Justice," "Environmental Politics," and so on.

Moreover, the disciplines of knowledge are not simply categories of "high culture" for children to absorb and accumulate; they are sources of insight and information that might be brought to bear on problems of living, lenses through which to look at those issues that confront us (Beane 1993). It is this last point that we can use to understand, for example, how talk about curriculum integration needs to move beyond mere questions about how to connect present pieces of the curriculum and become a larger conversation involving what those connections might be about. As Dewey (1938, p. 49) pointed out:

> What avail is it to win prescribed amounts of information about geography and history, to win ability to read and write, if in the process the individual loses his [sic] soul; loses his appreciation of things worthwhile, of the values to which these things are relative; if he loses desire to apply what he has learned and, above all, loses the ability to extract meaning from his future experiences as they occur.

Despite democratic claims about equal opportunity, many obstacles still block the path of nonprivileged young people in our schools—for instance, the overuse of standardized tests. One of the historic problems of many progressive curriculum ideas (and one reason they have often lacked support in nonprivileged communities) is that they appear to deemphasize the kind of official knowledge and skills that young people need to negotiate their way past the gatekeepers of socioeconomic access (Delpit 1986, 1988).

We previously noted that democratic schools are in part distinguished from other kinds of progressive schools in that they explicitly seek change in antidemocratic conditions in the school and society. Educators who work in democratic schools, however, are also acutely aware that such conditions, and the obstacles to larger access, must be reckoned with until they are changed. For this reason, a democratic curriculum seeks to help students become knowledgeable and skilled in many ways, including those required by the gatekeepers of socioeconomic access. In short, democratic educators live with the constant tension of seeking a more significant education for young people while still attending to the knowledge and skills expected by powerful educational forces whose interests are anything but democratic. Thus, we cannot ignore dominant knowledge. Having it does open some doors. But we must be careful in our interpretation here, because we do not want to endorse a continuation of the rigid "drill and skill" programs that so often constitute the school experiences of nonprivileged children. These children, too, have a right to the best of our progressive ideas. Our task is to reconstruct dominant knowledge and employ it to help, not hinder, those who are least privileged in this society.

The matter of creating a democratic curriculum is almost certain to involve conflict and contention. Practically all that is included in this sketch comes up against much of the dominant and longstanding view of what the planned curriculum ought to be about. The possibility of hearing a wide range of views and voices is often seen as a threat to the dominant culture, especially since some of those voices offer interpretations of issues and events quite different from those traditionally taught in schools. Worse yet, encouraging young people to critically analyze issues and events raises the possibility that they might call dominant interpretations (and teachings) into question. The same is true for organizing the curriculum around major social problems and issues, but this arrangement also comes into conflict with the sterilized version of knowledge and skill that is part of the separate-subject, discipline-centered, "high culture" approach to curriculum. And, finally, the possibility that young people might contribute their own questions and concerns to the curriculum raises the threat of touching on issues that reveal the ethical and political contradictions that permeate our society and of detracting from the values this society says it upholds.

All of these sources of resistance have been encountered repeatedly by those committed to democratic schooling. The resistance is not always couched in clear and explicit terms, however. For example, there are those who say that young people should not take on social issues because they are not ready to understand the complexities involved or because they might become depressed. Such arguments, of course, entirely ignore the fact that the young are real people living out real lives in our society; many of them know all too well, from their own lived experiences, about the consequences of racism, poverty, gender bias, homelessness, and so on. Obviously, then, those arguments simply seek to avoid the possibility that young people might come to see the political, ethical, and social contradictions that detract from their own dignity and seek to act against them.

It is important to note again that the concept of democratic schools is not intended only for the experiences of students. Adults, too, including professional educators, have a right to experience the democratic way of life in schools. We have already cited one example with regard to participation in determining policy and other decision making. But just as young people have a right to help create arrangements for their own education, so do teachers and other educators have a right to help create their own programs for professional growth based upon their perceptions of problems and issues in their classrooms, schools, and professional lives.

Furthermore, teachers have a right to have their voices heard in creating the curriculum, especially that intended for the particular young people they work with. Even the most casual of observers cannot help but notice that this right has been seriously eroded over the past several decades as curriculum decisions and even specific curriculum plans have been centralized in state and district offices of education. The consequent "de-skilling" of teachers, the redefinition of their work as the implementation of others' ideas and plans, is among the most obvious, and unbecoming, examples of how democracy has been dissolving in our schools (Apple 1986). Moreover, much of the talk about "site-based management," while appearing to reverse such centralization, actually amounts to little more than localizing struggles over limited resources and accountability for policy and program decisions made in distant places.

Finally, the matter of teachers' control of their own professional work involves not just resources and curriculum mandates, but instructional practices as well. Earlier we described how structural and curricular aspects of the school might be shaped by democratic values, though we also understand that they are also guided by research and other technical knowledge. In democratic schools, such knowledge does not come only from "elite" sources located outside the school, such as academic researchers. Of even more interest is the knowledge that teachers produce for their own use through action research and local dialogue. This does not mean other sources of professional knowledge are invalid or useless; it simply means they are not the only sources of worthwhile ideas.

When we link the democratic right of teachers to exercise meaningful control over their own work with the obligation of teachers and other adults to extend the democratic way of life to young people, we see the real possibility that democratic values might become a source of coherence for life in our schools. To turn the possibility into reality, however, we will again have to come up against some difficult questions. For instance, parents, the community, and the state certainly have a right to say what goals they want for education. But should they have the same say as professional educators in decisions about such matters as curriculum organization and resources? Does the heavy obligation to democracy that we have asked teachers to carry entitle them to certain professional autonomies beyond community control? What can the stories in this book tell us about such questions?

Building on a Rich Legacy

The picture we have sketched so far seems splendid in theory, but can it be fleshed out given present realities? It is true that the gap between democratic values and school practices is as wide now as it has ever been. But as the stories in this book reveal, the struggle to create democratic schools is alive in many places. The efforts described here are not anomalies of our own times; they are contemporary examples of a long line of work that has stretched over more than a century. As such, they offer a glimpse of the possibilities on the other side of the question that people today are still asking themselves: *How might schools both express and extend the meaning of democracy?*

We will read, for example, of serious efforts to connect the work of the school with the life of the community. Behind the projects described here lie movements that took place fifty and more years ago in places like Baltimore, Maryland, and Pulaski, Wisconsin, and Pasadena, California—places where young people undertook projects to solve serious community problems (see, for example, Anderson and Young 1951). Like today's efforts, those earlier projects were not short-term activities, important as those might be, but sustained efforts to forge substantive links with communities.

We will also read of attempts to create space in the curriculum for the study of large-scale social problems. Here we can look back to some of the progressive schools involved in the famous Eight-Year Study of the 1930s (Aikin 1962) and to the many classroom stories that emerged from the "core" movement in the 1940s and '50s (see, for example, Faunce and Bossing 1951).

And we will look at cooperative learning, which was favored in many of the earlier "core" schools and in the child-centered programs described by Rugg and Shumaker (1928) and the authors of *Life Skills in School and Society* (Rubin 1969). Our stories, like the earlier efforts, are concerned primarily with cooperative learning as a crucial aspect of the democratic way of life, not with the current popular focus of cooperative learning as a specific strategy for academic achievement.

In various ways, each story in this book emphasizes the involvement of young people in curriculum and other kinds of planning. The authors are following a long line of work describing such involvement not simply as a technique for reducing alienation and rebellion in classrooms but as part of a larger commitment to promoting individual and collective efficacy among young people (see, for example, Hopkins 1941; Giles, McCutchen, and Zechiel 1942; Zapf 1959; Waskin and Parrish 1967).

These stories also speak to serious efforts to build upon cultural diversity and to assuage the inequitable conditions surrounding cultural differences. In this regard, we should not forget that African Americans developed textbooks on their own history for segregated schools in the South during the 1930s and '40s. So much of the work in this area stands on the shoulders of W.E.B. Du Bois, who relentlessly fought to elevate the status and expectations of education for blacks—for example, seeing in job-skill training programs the obvious implications for differentiation of labor by race: "The ideals of education, whether men are taught to teach or plow, to weave or to write, must not be allowed to sink into sordid utilitarianism. Education must keep broad ideals before it, and never forget that it is dealing with Souls and not with Dollars" (Du Bois 1902, p. 82). We will hear the same theme resounding in the view of vocational education carried out at the Rindge School.

Nor are the authors here the first to recognize that creating democratic schools is a difficult endeavor when larger currents outside the school seem to be flowing in the opposite direction. Rugg and others (1939) spoke to this issue in the midst of social efficiency movements during the industrial revolution. And the authors of the 1952 ASCD Yearbook, *Growing Up in an Anxious Age* (Cunningham 1952), at the height of the McCarthy era, recounted chilling stories of ultraconservative attacks that resonate in our own times.

This brief historical sketch has focused mainly on the legacy of democratic education within schools. We would be remiss, however, if we failed to recognize that such work was (and still is) done in conjunction with efforts outside the schools themselves. For example, much of the impulse toward democratic schools rests on the prolific work of John Dewey, including not only that in education, such as his epic *Democracy and Education* (1916), but the vast array of essays and books on democracy in virtually all aspects of social affairs. A large debt is also owed to people like Elizabeth Harrison and Ella Flagg Young, who fought hard for the rights of children and teachers, and to others like George Counts and Harold Rugg, who advocated for a view of education as part of more widespread democratic social reconstruction.

Similarly, political activists in larger civil rights movements played no small part in democratizing various aspects of schooling. Were it not for their efforts, the schools might still be plagued by legally sanctioned racial segregation and exclusion of people with disabilities. As well, we cannot ignore the efforts of such groups as the American Library Association to protect young people from the restrictive limitations of censorship. While the courts are still confounded by the question of whether the school should be an arena for full democracy or a "limited forum" for democratic rights, it is all too possible to imagine that the question itself might never have reached the courts were it not for the relentless appeals of democratic activists.

Clearly, then, the idea of extending and protecting democracy in schools is not simply a product of our own times. Both the general concept and the specific features we have sketched out have roots in efforts stretching back more than a century. The historian of democratic schools, however, always has to keep two things in mind. First, just as democracy has had multiple meanings in the larger society, so has its interpretation with regard to schools been somewhat ambiguous. Second, democracy is a dynamic concept that requires continuous examination in light of changing times. For these reasons, we are always at risk of being disappointed when one or another historical attempt at democratic schools did not push as far as we would wish or is revealed as a mix of success and contradiction. What is important is that we recognize moments of democratic impulse in the past as a legacy on which to build our own efforts.

Toward Democratic Schools

We have chosen to include in this book four examples of democracy brought to life in schools: Central Park East Secondary School in New York City, the Rindge School of Technical Arts in the Boston area, La Escuela Fratney in Milwaukee, and a particular program within Marquette Middle School (now called Georgia O'Keefe Middle School) in Madison, Wisconsin. Each represents the creative response of educators to the realities of poverty, injustice, and dislocation. And all show the rich learning experiences that result from people's determination to make their classrooms centers of democratic practice and to create permeable boundaries between the school and the larger society.

Early on, we made a decision that these stories must be told in the words of the people involved. This is crucial. The feelings of frustration, and sometimes cynicism, that many educators and community members experience are often the result of not hearing each others' stories. Failure seems to make better headlines than hard-won, slow success. The stories presented here are not romantic. They are honest about the possibilities, and difficulties, we face as we move toward more democratic practices.

And let us remember who that "we" is. Democratic schools need to be based on a broad definition of "we," a commitment to building a community that is both of the school and of the society in which the school exists. Taken together, the stories told in this book say something quite important about the realities of democratic school reform. In each case, success required the conscious building of coalitions within the school and between the school and constituencies outside it. In none of the cases was the impetus generated from the "top." Instead, bottom-up movements—groups of teachers, the community, social activists, and so on—provided the driving force for change. Finally, none of the reforms was driven by a technical, achievement-at-all-costs vision. Instead, each was linked to a broadly defined set of values that was put into practice: enhancing participation at the grass roots and in the school, empowering individuals and groups who had heretofore been largely silenced, creating new ways of linking the real world and real social problems with the school so that the school is integrally connected to the experiences of people in their daily lives.

We shall be honest here. None of the examples included in this book is guaranteed to solve all the many problems schools confront. In fact, given the economic and social crises that continue to beset so many people in this society, schools and classrooms such as these have their work cut out for them, not only educationally but economically as well (see, for example, Kozol 1991). By attempting to create new, more democratic possibilities in our public schools, however, we can relearn what is possible. Make no mistake about it, the stakes are high, as James Mursell (1955, p. 3) pointed out 40 years ago:

> If the schools of a democratic society do not exist for and work for the support and extension of democracy, then they are either socially useless or socially dangerous. At the best they will educate people who will go their way and earn their living indifferent to the obligations of citizenship in particular and of the democratic way of life in general. . . . But quite likely they will educate people to be enemies of democracy—people who will fall prey to demagogues, and who back movements and rally round leaders hostile to the democratic way of life. Such schools are either futile or subversive. They have no legitimate reason for existence.

References

Aikin, Wilford. (1962). *The Story of the Eight-Year Study.* New York: Harper and Brothers.

Anderson, Walter A., and William E. Young, eds. (1951). *Action for Curriculum Improvement.* Washington, D.C.: ASCD.

Apple, Michael. (1986). *Teachers and Texts: A Political Economy of Class and Gender Relations in Schools.* New York and London: Routledge and Kegan Paul.

Apple, Michael. (1988). "Redefining Equality." *Teachers College Record* 90: 167–184.

Apple, Michael. (1990). *Ideology and Curriculum.* 2nd ed. New York: Routledge.

Apple, Michael. (1993). *Official Knowledge: Democratic Education in a Conservative Age.* New York: Routledge.

Beane, James. (1990). *Affect in the Curriculum.* New York: Teachers College Press.

Beane, James. (1993). *A Middle School Curriculum: From Rhetoric to Reality.* 2nd ed. Columbus, Ohio: National Middle School Association.

Bastian, Ann, Norm Fruchter, Marilyn Gittell, Colin Greer, and Kenneth Haskins. (1986). *Choosing Equality: The Case for Democratic Schooling.* Philadelphia: Temple University Press.

Cunningham, Ruth, ed. (1952). *Growing Up in an Anxious Age.* Washington, D.C.: ASCD.

Delfattore, Joan. (1993). *Why Johnny Can't Read.* New Haven: Yale University Press.

Delpit, Lisa. (1986). "Skills and Other Dilemmas of a Progressive Black Educator." *Harvard Educational Review* 56: 379–385.

Delpit, Lisa. (1988). "The Silenced Dialogue: Power and Pedagogy in Educating Other People's Children." *Harvard Educational Review* 58: 280–298.

Dewey, John. (1916). *Democracy and Education.* New York: Macmillan.

Dewey, John. (1938). *Experience and Education.* Bloomington, Ind.: Kappa Delta Pi.

Du Bois, W.E.B. (1906). *The Negro Artisan.* Atlanta: Atlanta University Press.

Faunce, Roland, and Nelson Bossing. (1951). *Developing the Core Curriculum.* New York: Prentice-Hall.

Giles, H.H., S.F. McCutchen, and A.N. Zechiel. (1942). *Exploring the Curriculum.* New York and London: Harper and Brothers.

Graebner, William. (1988). *The Engineering of Consent: Democracy as Social Authority in the Twentieth Century.* Madison: University of Wisconsin Press.

Greene, Maxine. (1985). "The Role of Education in Democracy." *Educational Horizons* 63 (Special Issue): 3–9.

Gutmann, Amy. (1987). *Democratic Education.* Princeton, N.J.: Princeton University Press.

Hopkins, L. Thomas. (1941). *Interaction: The Democratic Process.* Boston: D.C. Heath.

Jensen, Carl, and Project Censored. (1994). *Censored: The News That Didn't Make the News—and Why.* New York: Four Walls Eight Windows.

Kozol, Jonathan. (1991). *Savage Inequalities.* New York: Crown.

Ladson-Billings, Gloria. (in press). "Making Math Meaningful in Cultural Contests." In *New Directions in Equity for Mathematics Instruction,* edited by Walter Secada, Elizabeth Fennema, and Lisa Byrd. New York: Cambridge University Press.

Miel, Alice, and Kimball Wiles, eds. (1949.) *Toward Better Teaching: A Report of Current Practices.* Washington, D.C.: ASCD.

Mursell, James. (1955). *Principles of Democratic Education.* New York: Norton.

Oakes, Jeannie. (1985). *Keeping Track: How Schools Structure Inequality.* New Haven: Yale University Press.

Rubin, Louis J., ed. (1969). *Life Skills in School and Society.* Washington, D.C.: ASCD.

Rugg, Harold, ed. (1939). *Democracy and the Curriculum.* Third Yearbook of the John Dewey Society. New York: D. Appleton-Century.

Rugg, Harold, and Anne Shumaker. (1928). *The Child-Centered School.* New York: World Book.

Waskin, Yvonne, and Louise Parrish. (1967). *Teacher-Pupil Planning for Better Classroom Learning.* New York: Pitman.

Williams, Raymond. (1961). *The Long Revolution.* London: Chatto and Windus.

Wood, George. (1988). "Democracy and the Curriculum." In *The Curriculum: Problems, Politics, and Possibilities,* edited by Landon Beyer and Michael Apple. Albany: State University of New York Press.

Wood, George. (1992). *Schools That Work.* New York: Dutton.

Zapf, Rosalind. (1959). *Democratic Practices in the Secondary School.* Englewood Cliffs, N.J.: Prentice-Hall.

2

Central Park East Secondary School: The Hard Part Is Making It Happen

DEBORAH MEIER AND PAUL SCHWARZ

Introduction

Central Park East Secondary School (CPESS), an alternative high school, expands on the successful learning environment created at the Central Park East Elementary Schools over the last 20 years. The secondary school is a cooperative project of Community School Board #4, the New York City Board of Education Alternative High School Division, and the Coalition of Essential Schools, a national high school network.

CPESS was started in the fall of 1985 with 80 7th graders. The school currently enrolls 450 students in grades 7–12 and although CPESS will not grow larger, we have begun the creation of 11 new Coalition high schools in New York City. The students who attend CPESS are mostly neighborhood (East Harlem) residents. Eighty-five percent of the students are African American or Latino, and more than 20 percent are eligible for service provided by special education. From careful tracking of our students, even when they move and attend other schools, we know that 97.3 percent of the students who have attended CPESS graduated from high school. And 90 percent of those graduates attended college.

The fundamental aim of CPESS is to teach students to use their minds well, to prepare them for a well-lived life that is productive, socially useful, and personally satisfying. The school's academic program stresses intellectual achievement and emphasizes the mastery of a limited

26

number of centrally important subjects. This program goes hand in hand with an approach that emphasizes learning how to learn, how to reason, and how to investigate complex issues that require collaboration and personal responsibility.

The final high school diploma is not based on time spent in class or Carnegie units, but on each student's clear demonstration of achievement through the presentation of 14 portfolios to a graduation committee. The school's values include high expectations, trust, a sense of personal decency, and respect for diversity. The school is open to all students and expects a lot from each student.

The school is guided by the principles of the Coalition of Essential Schools, a national organization of high schools directed by Ted Sizer. The Coalition's principles include:

1. *Less is more.* It is more important to know some things well than to know many things superficially.

2. *Personalization.* Although the course of study is unified and universal, teaching and learning are personalized. No teacher is responsible for teaching more than 80 students (40 at CPESS) or advising more than 15.

3. *Goal Setting.* High standards are set for all students. Students must clearly exhibit mastery of their school work.

4. *Student as Worker.* CPESS teachers "coach" students, encouraging them to find answers and, in effect, to teach themselves. Thus, students discover answers and solutions and learn by doing rather than by simply repeating what textbooks (or teachers) say.

Habits of Mind, Work, and Heart

It was Friday, May 2, 1992. Our students had spent the week talking, organizing, and dealing with powerful feelings in the wake of the Rodney King verdict and the riots in Los Angeles. As luck would have it, an all-white choir from a small Michigan town was scheduled to sing for us that day. While L.A. was burning, and probably scared to death, the choir faced an audience of mostly African American and Latino teenagers, many still brimming with eagerness to protest. There was tension in the air as one of our seniors stepped up to ask if he could say a few words that he thought might help.

"I took it on myself to come up here and talk to all you students about what we've been going through. I know from the Senior Institute that a lot of students have been talking about what's been going on in L.A., and it bothers them a lot.

"I just wanted to tell you that no one here is our enemy . . . and that we have to stick together.

" . . . and that there's lots of people from . . . Michigan, right?" The students laugh. "Michigan, not California, right?" There is more laughter from students.

"What they are doing here, they are doing for us. They are not here to make us feel better. They are here because they like to sing, and they're here to show us what they've got.

"They are not our enemies either. There is no one in this room that is our enemy. If we can stick together and stay with each other, we can show these people that we are not falling apart like some other people are." Cheers and whoops fill the room.

"You got to do what you got to do, but showing your anger at these people here isn't going to do anything for any of us."

If the primary public responsibility and justification for tax-supported schooling is raising a generation of fellow citizens, then the school—of necessity—must be a place where students learn the habits of mind, work, and heart that lie at the core of such a democracy.

Since you can't learn to be good at something you've never experienced—even vicariously—then it stands to reason that schools are a good place to experience what such democratic habits might be. It's as simple as that, and as complex. You can't learn to play a game you've never seen played. No one would think of raising up musicians without being sure to place them in the company of musicians, including some at the top of their art.

Our task at CPESS was to take this idea seriously once again, and return the business of rearing our young to such basic principles. Instead of placing students in cohorts of equal ignorance and creating settings in which no expert ever performed his or her craft in the presence of novices and in which no one, novice or expert, ever showed what they could do, but only talked about it, we tried to turn the tables on it all.

We'd keep the idea of kindergarten, where we both began our careers, going all the way through high school—and long after, we hoped. We wanted a schoolhouse that was naturally organized to be interesting, just like a good kindergarten room. We wanted a place where young people and their teachers could work in shared ways around topics and materials they were inclined to enjoy, for long stretches of time, and without too many preconceived strictures. We wanted opportunities for the least expert to watch and observe the more expert, and then to practice out at their own pace. We wanted settings in which people knew each other through each other's works, through the close observation of actual practice—by our teacher colleagues and our student colleagues. A truly collegial setting.

So, we knew we had to be small, multi-aged, intimate, and interesting. Family and school would need to be allies, as the two institutions responsible for shared child-rearing tasks. Between us, we had to find ways to make the idea of growing up seem wonderful and enticing, and noticeably varied enough to include everyone. We had to make the idea of being a powerful citizen on an ever broadening platform, with the capacity to play effective roles both in public and private, seem feasible and imaginable and appealing.

That's what good schooling could do. But it took taking apart all this large and wordy rhetoric and finding the details that counted, just as we had both done when we daily set about putting together our kindergarten classrooms, from the block corner to the sand table, the selection of particular books, the organizing of pencils and paints, the placement of works of art, always with particular children in mind, always with particular purposes in mind.

So we put together CPESS, over time, collectively, modifying as we went, mindful of all the details of a place filled with many stories as well as common purposes. We created a structure in which people—students and students, students and teachers, and teachers and teachers, and their families—could think aloud together and jointly make decisions. We had to define what "using your mind well," the Coalition of Essential Schools' overarching mission, meant. What were the habits of mind that defined a democratic citizen? We thought of friends who were "good citizens" and tried to imagine what it was that they had in common. Surely it wasn't the ability to recall some body of facts or information, although they were curious about such mundane details. The two qualities that seemed to define our ideal citizen were *empathy* and *skepticism:*

the ability to see a situation from the eyes of another and the tendency to wonder about the validity of what we encountered.

Our operational definition of a thoughtful person, a person whom we would be proud to claim as a graduate of our school, was one who could demonstrate to us, in a variety of ways and in numerous disciplines, that he or she was in the habit of tackling the following five questions:

- How do you know what you know? (Evidence)
- From whose viewpoint is this being presented? (Perspective)
- How is this event or work connected to others? (Connections)
- What if things were different? (Supposition)
- Why is this important? (Relevance)

We have organized our curriculum and our assessment around the idea that a person in the habit of looking for answers to these five questions when presented with a novel situation is using his or her mind well. The nuances, the vocabulary, the tools change from physics to literature to geometry and so on. If these questions are the right ones, however, they ought also to apply to the playground and the workplace. Of course, such habits are neither learned nor used in a vacuum. They are embedded in appropriate subject matter; they depend on the ability of the learner to use skills of reading, writing, logic, computation, research, and scientific inquiry to give them substance. But we hold to the concept of their universality across subject matter and age. A person in the habit of asking these five questions is a thoughtful person.

In fact, the biggest step we took was deciding that a student would graduate CPESS almost entirely on the basis of evidence of such thoughtfulness, over and over again in 14 designated fields of work. We called this Graduation by Portfolio, although our portfolios are compilations not merely of written work, but of everything and anything students believe speaks to their meeting the graduation standards we have spelled out.

We invented graduation committees, which are a little like doctoral committees. Each committee includes at least two faculty members, an adult of the student's choice, and another student member. Their job is to read, review, observe, listen to the evidence, and make appropriate recommendations for revision or approval. When we started, it was hard for us to imagine such a process. But today stories like the one beginning on page 33 reinforce our commitment to this time-consuming process.

The 14 Portfolio Areas:
An Overview for Students and Parents

The primary responsibility of the Senior Institute student is to complete the 14 portfolio requirements listed below.

These portfolios reflect cumulative knowledge and skill in each area as well as the specific CPESS habits of mind and work. Students will present the work in all 14 portfolio areas to their Graduation Committee for review and acceptance. They will meet for a full review of their seven chosen "majors" to present, discuss, and defend their work. There are, therefore, two stages to keep in mind: (1) preparation of the portfolio materials in collaboration with the advisor and others, and (2) presentation and defense of the materials. In some cases, portfolio work will need to be expanded, modified, and represented for final approval. Students may also choose to present work a second time to earn a higher assessment.

It is important to remember that a majority of the work done in connection with a portfolio can and should be the outcome of the courses, seminars, internships, and independent study that a student has engaged in during the normal course of his or her Senior Institute years. In addition, some of the material may be an outgrowth of work initiated in Divisions I or II or, where appropriate (e.g., the Language Other Than English portfolio), work completed prior to entering the Senior Institute.

Portfolios include work in 14 areas: seven "majors" and seven "minors." There is no one way to complete these requirements, nor one way to present them. People are different, and the individual portfolio will reflect these differences. The term "portfolio" covers all the ways in which a student exhibits his or her knowledge, understanding, and skill. CPESS recommends interdisciplinary studies wherever possible, so work completed to meet one requirement may be used to fulfill other requirements as well.

While the final review is based on individual accomplishment, almost all portfolio requirements can be based on work done in collaboration with others, including group presentations. Such collaborative work is encouraged, since it often enables a student to engage in a much more complex and interesting project.

Quality and depth of understanding, good use of CPESS's five habits of mind, and the capacity to present competent and convincing evidence of mastery as relevant to each particular field are the major criteria used by the Graduation Committee; however, portfolio work must reflect a concern for both substance and style. For example, written work must be submitted in clear, grammatical English that reflects the expected proficiency level of a high school graduate in spelling, grammar, and legibility. Errors should be eliminated before the portfolio is presented to the committee. Written work must generally be submitted in typewritten form. The same care in preparation and presentation applies to all other forms of work. Portfolio work should represent a student's best effort. The same holds true for the manner of presentation.

(continued)

Different characteristics are more or less relevant to each portfolio area. Each academic discipline, for example, has developed its own "scoring grid" to help students and Graduation Committee members focus objectively on the appropriate criteria. Over time, the criteria for acceptable performance will be more fully developed through both the creation of new scoring grids and the compilation of past student work that demonstrates accepted levels of skill. Students are expected to become familiar with the criteria by which they are measured (both the scoring grids and former student work).

At Graduation Committee meetings, students should be prepared to discuss not only the content of the portfolio, but their computer knowledge and growth in particular fields of work.

The following are the 14 Portfolio areas:

1. Postgraduate Plan
2. Science/Technology*
3. Mathematics*
4. History *and Social Studies**
5. Literature*
6. Autobiography
7. School and Community Service and Internship
8. Ethics and Social Issues
9. Fine Arts/Aesthetics
10. Practical Skills
11. Media
12. Geography
13. Language Other Than English/Dual Language Proficiency
14. Physical Challenge

Senior Project

One of the above portfolio topics or items will be separately assessed as a final Senior project. Each student is required to make a major presentation in 7 of the 14 areas described above. These include the four starred Portfolios, and at least three others chosen in cooperation with the advisor. Grades of Distinguished, SatPlus, Sat, or MinSat will be used to grade work as a whole. In the seven "minor" portfolios, a student will be graded pass/fail. Passing will be upon recommendation of the advisor and approval of the full Graduation Committee.

The student may, however, request a grade from the advisor (Distinguished, SatPlus, etc.). In this case, the student must provide the committee with sufficient time to review all relevant materials and to discuss the recommended grade at a meeting of the committee. Such a grade would be subject to approval by the entire committee.

A Meeting of the Graduation Committee

It is a warm Friday afternoon in September and Monique's graduation committee has convened for the first time. As we wait for Monique's mother to arrive (each student is allowed to choose one adult, and Monique has chosen her mother—according to local wisdom, always a risky choice). Monique is so nervous she can't sit still. "I've got to go to the bathroom," she says, and makes her third trip in the last 15 minutes.

Finally, we all settle in around a table in my office and Monique begins her presentation. She has chosen to present a paper on AIDS discrimination in health care. She refers to her paper, but only occasionally. At the start, she is somewhat ashen-faced. She sits bolt upright, as opposed to her usual adolescent slump, and begins nearly every sentence with "I put . . . "—as in "I put in an interview with a nurse who works in the emergency room to describe the feelings of a professional whose primary responsibility is not AIDS-related."

Monique finishes her presentation and asks if there are any questions. She knows there will be. This is the part of the meeting where committee members probe to see if she has acquired our five habits of mind, the hallmark of a CPESS graduate. We begin gently asking her for the source of some of her information. She handles these questions easily. Students always discuss committee experiences with their friends, and Monique expected questions about sources.

But the questions quickly become less predictable. "Monique," I ask, "you spoke of doctors who screened patients for the HIV virus without their knowledge or permission. You see this as a bad thing, an invasion of their privacy. Just last Sunday I saw a TV program about Cuba and their response to the AIDS epidemic. In Cuba they test everyone. They don't ask permission. When they find an HIV-positive person, they quarantine them. They are put in a comfortable place with good food and excellent health care, but they must stay there. Period. One result is that they have greatly lessened the spread of the disease. What if they were to do that here?"

Monique is on her own here. She certainly did not anticipate this question, and she can't begin her answer with "I put." But something happens to her at that moment; a physical change takes place, one that I've often seen at a graduation committee meeting. Monique doesn't hesitate. She straightens up, leans forward, looks me right in the eye, and says, "My father died of AIDS and that's why I decided to present this portfolio first. It is real important to me."

She continues, "I would be in favor of anything that prevents AIDS or even slows it down a little bit, but I don't know about not telling people that you are testing them. I can see both sides of the question and I don't want to decide. I think we should take a vote."

"Who should vote?" I ask.

"Everyone," she answers immediately. "Even little kids. This is so important that everyone should be able to vote."

The committee meeting ends after an hour of presentation and questions. Committee members fill out grids that we have created here at CPESS: one to assess the major project in the portfolio (our portfolios are compilations of work) and a tabulation form that gives a grade for this portfolio, her first of seven major portfolios.

As I announce the grade to Monique—a better than satisfactory grade—and give her our feedback on what we thought was strong in her work and what we thought might have improved the portfolio, she grins from ear to ear. She is back to her younger self. She can hardly listen to us and immediately excuses herself to go and talk to Yuiza and Frances, her best friends, who are waiting in the lobby for her.

I put papers and forms and tabulation sheets away and prepare for my next graduation committee. Carlos is presenting his literature portfolio—or rather, he is presenting himself as a person in the habit of using his mind well, of using our habits of mind, and he is going to demonstrate these qualities through his work in the field of literature.

After school, I meet some school friends and they ask me why I am so "high." It is because occasionally, during committee meetings like Monique's, I witness the fruits of our work together. I see the hidden hours of struggle that so many teachers and parents and students have invested in learning. The committee meetings are not only our final assessment, they are often "payoff time," a concrete reward for having studied and read and written and argued and thought so long and so hard.

And once in a while I see magic. Not sleight-of-hand magic, but the magic of a child's first step or her first word. Magic that has been earned. The magic of students growing up as thinkers, gaining confidence, showing off their minds—of a young person changing, in front of my eyes, into a woman who is confident, thoughtful, and competent.

The Choices We Have Made

How did we create graduation committees as rigorous and as personal as the one described above? How did we create a school organization that allows teachers to attend to details, the way early childhood teachers do? The changes we have made are not simple. They have forced us to make weighty choices, and there have been sacrifices involved in each of them.

Half-Day, Theme-Centered Classes

CPESS offers a common core curriculum for all students in grades 7 through 10, organized around two major fields: math/science for half the school day and humanities (art, history, social studies, and literature) for the other half.

Each class is centered around a theme. Here, for example, are two themes of study, one in humanities and one in math/science, both taken from the curriculum of our Division II, 9th and 10th grades:

Justice: Systems of Laws and Government. At least two very different concepts of justice are explored in this year-long theme: one consensual and the other adversarial. Ideas of fairness, conflict resolution, and equity are examined in these two societies. The American justice system and critical legal landmarks are examined in detail. Students develop first-hand experience with the preparation and defense of a legal brief. They explore the jury system and the nature of evidence. The essential questions in the study are: How is authority justified? How are conflicts resolved? Are justice, morality, and fairness synonymous?

Motion and Forces of Energy is a two-year theme driven by the following essential questions: How do things move? How does energy behave in its different forms? Is energy ever made or lost? In the investigation of these questions, students work on projects such as designing and analyzing an original amusement park ride or doing a scientific analysis of a projectile (e.g., a basketball or a javelin in flight). They used a variety of commercially produced computer software to model and analyze projectile motion and collisions of two or more bodies. The theme includes an emphasis on the scientific method and the techniques of statistics and probability. Students also investigate the mathematical themes of counting, measuring, locating, and describing, which lead them to a more intense study of algebra, geometry, trigonometry, mathematical transformations, vectors, and matrices.

In grades 7 through 10, each class period is two hours long, and each teacher teaches two classes a day rather than the five classes that are common in many other schools. This change has meant a reconceptualization of instructional practice. Two-hour classes push teachers to use a variety of strategies, such as whole-group instruction, small-group collaborative work, library research, and hands-on problem solving. The teacher can't bore kids by lecturing them for two hours at a time.

Instruction in the Senior Institute—our name for grades 11 and 12—works a little differently. Students in this transitional stage spend more time taking courses out of our building: at colleges and museums, at internships, and in independent study. A substantial portion of their day is also spent with their advisors, preparing for graduation and the steps beyond.

Small Classes

A second priority is to reduce not only the number of classes taught, but also class size. To accomplish this goal, we have chosen to concentrate the great bulk of the resources allotted to us in core classroom instruction. As we have grown from a single 7th grade class in 1985 to our full complement today, we have made the ratio of students to teachers our priority. We have no guidance counselors, no gym teacher (although we do have an extensive intramural program and a substantial after-school athletic program), no music teacher, and a single art teacher for the whole school. We have no department chairs, no deans, and one social worker; in return for class sizes of under 20, other teachers have assumed many of the functions traditionally carried out by these personnel. All professional staff are advisors to a group of under 15 students for two years. This group meets for several hours each week, and it is the advisor who has long-range, in-depth relationships with each student's family.

Critical Friends

Powerful as this educational process is, it puts us at odds with ideas of curriculum and assessment that stress memorization and coverage. This kind of learning is personal; it requires internalizing, not just saying, difficult ideas. It assumes an active role by the learner and, like other creative acts, it is unpredictable and full of surprises. No textbooks or standardized tests exist for teaching this way. Adults must work together to constantly re-create curriculum, invent new forms for exhibiting knowledge, and decide when the school is ready to say, "She's done it. It's time to hand her a diploma." Such chutzpa requires that standards be constantly discussed and agreed on.

External colleagues, what we call "critical friends," are essential to help us look critically at the school's work. "Autonomy" can't be synonymous with privacy. Quite the opposite. CPESS, and its work, are always public. We bring in experts of various sorts several times a year to help us set standards and examine our curriculum. For instance, professors from local colleges and universities have come to our school and reviewed the writing quality of portfolio items, in almost all cases confirming our staff's own evaluations of the items. And we've even had critical friends join us for a full day of graduation portfolio review. These teachers from traditional public schools in New York City, state education department employees, principals of comprehensive high schools, principals and teachers from our sister schools, foundation representatives, and outside experts looked at portfolios of differing quality, talked to students about their studies, and watched videotapes of student presentations. They also met with us and with teachers, offering thought-provoking comments, criticisms, and advice on a range of topics, from the structure of our school to academic requirements. By opening our program to this kind of outside scrutiny, we hold ourselves accountable to the public while also providing rich collaborative experiences for the staff.

Time for Planning, Collaboration, and Assessment

To make such collaboration possible we had to address another priority: teacher time. We had to build into the professional life of teachers time for adults to do this new kind of planning, collaboration, and assessment. Every Monday, staff meet from 3:00 to 4:30. On Friday, we have classes from 8:00 to 1:00, and the staff meet again from 1:30 until 3:00. This is three hours a week that staff work together on whole-school issues. Some of that time is used by vertical teams (all the humanities teachers and all the math/science teachers) to meet and discuss scope and sequence and standards of work from 7th grade through graduation. At least once a month, our whole staff gather to discuss issues of race, class, and gender. And once a month, we gather to consider school matters such as family conferences, report writing or reports, and recommendations from various working subgroups. Several times a year, we meet over weekends for public review of students' work and developing curriculum. We've even raised some funds to pay teachers a stipend for working during July on collaborative projects.

In addition, each week we have carved out a three-hour block of time for teams of teachers who work with the same students to meet. We have done this by requiring that each student in grades 7 through 10 have a community service placement. We have one teacher who is responsible for these placements. We organize the placements so that students who go into the community to work do so in constellations of 80 students per day. This arrangement frees teams of teachers to work together for that half day. The students check in with their advisor at 9:00 a.m. and then go to their placement. They return at noon and go to lunch and midday options (gym, library, etc). Their teachers have until 1:00 to plan collaboratively, and the students have rich opportunities for using their minds in a wide variety of institutions, from day-care classrooms to museums, hospitals, and homes for the aged.

These formal and informal gatherings that take place all day long are where "staff development" occurs. They are where the newest teacher learns his or her trade, and senior staff reexamine and revisit old issues. While everyone complains occasionally of being exhausted—and so we skip a meeting here and there—we don't complain of burnout. We're never treated like appliances, but are in control of our own profession.

Through these varied forms of face-to-face meetings, the governance of the school is enacted. Decisions are made, wherever possible, by those who must implement them. But decisions also belong to the wider community of staff, parents, and students, and they have always the right to ask that a decision be reconsidered, defended, and explained. In these open and accessible ways, staff and students learn about the complexities of democracy. They learn of its limitations and of the realities of institutional trade-offs. And they imagine how they might even do it better. We ourselves are forever tinkering with ways to govern better (and less), using the same habits of mind we ask of our students.

Altered Perceptions

We come back to the personal (as former kindergarten teachers, we couldn't do otherwise), which includes looking at children as members of their family and reflecting on how schooling has altered both children's and family's perceptions of themselves. One mother described to an audience of teachers how this kind of schooling has changed her family; her words convey what it is we hope for from our schooling:

> As we (our family) became familiar with the process of presenting work for criticism to a supportive group of peers, we all became involved with it.

> I remember when Zawadi (my middle daughter) was doing a portfolio item on Philip Parnell, a case of a teenager who was shot down and killed by a police officer in New Jersey. I went to the library with her and we did extensive research. She told me what to look for.

> She interviewed my brother, who is a NYC police officer, so she could get a feeling for what a police officer feels like when something like that happens. She didn't want her exhibition to be biased . . .

> I watched her formulate her questions. I watched her interview people. I watched her over a period of several years pull all that information into a play that she decided to use a vehicle for her presentation.

> And then I watched her have her friends from school come to my living room. I watched her become the director. And I watched her listen to them—to take into account how they felt—how they would have responded in that case.

> My son chose to focus on his experience as a child living in three different states and how they impacted on who he has become.

> This having to define himself was insightful to us all. His accounts of specific instances of racism were validated by his sisters and led to family discussions about those instances and how they could be empowering if you change the anger to strength.

> My youngest daughter has taken to documenting the family history, which has brought into the picture the total United States history and the history of the Caribbean. She has had to do extensive research

around those oral histories, which are important to me because I grew
up with them but never thought to document them. This process
allowed her to do that and to give her the time so that she wasn't doing
the rote kind of work our children used to do, but she was placing her
time in something that was meaningful and important to her, and she
was excited about that.

The history of progressive education has largely been written in
schools for young children—in kindergartens and early childhood centers and Head Start centers. Its spokespeople have been professionals
who have studied and practiced their craft with the young. Maria Mon-
tessori, Jean Piaget, John Dewey, Lillian Weber and Barbara Biber, and
so many other teachers who have gone before. They created schools
where what students studied was intimately connected to their lives, and
where people had a chance to work and learn side by side. Our success
at CPESS is to re-create those structures and to implement goals in
settings where older students learn. It is also our challenge.

We have created a structure where it is possible to learn to know
students well so they can learn to use their minds well; we have created
a structure where teachers can be in responsible control of their professional lives and where there is a strong professional community supporting them; we have created an assessment system that can hold students
to high standards without standardization; we have created a curriculum
structure based on habits of mind that focus on tools for thinking, not
just bits and pieces of information. That's the easy part; the hard part is
making it happen.

3

Beyond the Shop: Reinventing Vocational Education

LARRY ROSENSTOCK AND ADRIA STEINBERG

Vocational education straddles a fundamental contradiction. On the one hand it has long been, and still is, a means of providing an education to students who would not otherwise attend school. On the other hand, it has created a dual system in which lower income students are tracked into vocational classes and away from the academic courses that prepare other students for further education and higher income, white-collar jobs.

The Rindge School of Technical Arts opened in 1888 as the first public vocational high school in Massachusetts, and the second in the United States. Built with funds provided by a local industrialist named Frederick Rindge, the school still displays his sentiments, carved in granite over the front door: "Work is one of our greatest blessings. Everyone should have an honest occupation." Frederick Rindge acted out of a democratic impulse, yet helped create a mechanism for the "sorting of students by their evident and probable destinies" (Carnoy and Levin 1985, p. 94).

The groundwork for Rindge's generous bequest had been laid 50 years earlier in Massachusetts, when the State Board of Education, led by Horace Mann, argued that the Common School system should be expanded to bring together in the schools children from all backgrounds. Concerned that many rural and working-class families still did not send their children to school, local boards sought to differentiate the types of schools available. The introduction of vocational schools with agricultural and mechanical programs was described as providing a practical reason for Irish immigrant and rural students to attend.

By the 1880s and '90s, secondary schools were increasingly viewed as avenues to middle management jobs in the new industrial firms. Aware of the increasing strength of organized labor, the business sector sought to create programs that would train students in the new technical skills needed by industry, instill in them attitudes of loyalty to their employers, and socialize them for an industrial economy. Thus emerged in Massachusetts the first dual system: one to educate middle- and upper-level managers, the other to train laborers and clerical workers.

Despite criticism of the narrow, utilitarian nature of vocational education, it continued to spread, advocated by the newly formed National Association of Manufacturers and opposed initially by organized labor. A 1906 report by the Massachusetts Commission on Industrial and Technical Education triggered a debate between John Dewey and David Snedden, the Commissioner of Education in Massachusetts. While Snedden defended the efficiency of the dual system, Dewey saw the segregated vocational education favored by business as a "form of class education which would make the schools a more efficient agency for the reproduction of an undemocratic society" (Westbrook 1991, p. 175). Dewey viewed the issue of vocational education as central to the future of democracy; his framing of the issue still resonates strongly today:

> Its [vocational education's] right development will do more to make public education truly democratic than any other agency now under consideration. Its wrong treatment will as surely accentuate all undemocratic tendencies in our present situation, by fostering and strengthening class divisions in school and out. . . . Those who believe in the continued existence of what they are pleased to call the "lower classes" or the "laboring classes" would naturally rejoice to have schools in which these "classes" would be segregated. And some employers of labor would doubtless rejoice to have schools, supported by public taxation, supply them with additional food for their mills. . . . [Everyone else] should be united against every proposition, in whatever form advanced, to separate training of employees from training for citizenship, training of intelligence and character from training for narrow, industrial efficiency (Dewey in press).

Although there was deep disagreement about the direction of vocational education, it nevertheless had wide support. A powerful lobbying organization, the National Society for the Promotion of Industrial Education, was supported by a broad range of groups, including educators, the Chamber of Commerce, the National Association of Manufacturers, the American Federation of Labor (sensing the inevitability of vocational education, labor wanted a voice in redirecting its anti-union bias), major farm organizations, and settlement workers.

The campaign culminated in the passage of the Smith-Hughes Act in 1917, which began the federal support for vocational education that has continued until the present. The fundamental contradiction of vocational education was set: while it profoundly transformed the rate of Massachusetts high school enrollment from a mere 6.7 percent of 14- to 17-year-olds in 1888 to 32.3 percent of that population by 1906 (Krug 1969, p. 220, quoting the 1906 Report of the Massachusetts Commission on Industrial and Technical Education), it became a separate, second-class system under separate control. (Dewey's advocacy of a single system won a Pyrrhic victory: vocational education was incorporated into the public school system, but as a distinct track within that system.)

The segregation of vocational education was further reinforced by two other concomitant factors. The first, the compulsory education laws of 1923, captured into vocational programs many young people who were now required to go to school. At the same time, "intelligence tests" such as the IQ and Binet were developed and used to channel students toward either vocational or academic concentrations.

By the time of the authorization of the Carl D. Perkins Vocational Education and Applied Technology Act of 1990, Congress was receptive to the idea of substantially reshaping vocational education. Widespread dissatisfaction with the job entrance rates and wage rates of vocational school graduates, combined with strong pressure from a coalition of national advocacy groups led by the Center for Law and Education,[1] galvanized support for change. With only 27 percent of all vocational school graduates working for even a single day in a job related to their vocational training (*National Assessment of Vocational Education* 1987),

---

[1]The Center for Law and Education, based in Cambridge, Massachusetts, and Washington, D.C., advocates for the educational rights of low-income students and parents throughout the United States. Paul Weckstein, codirector of the center, was a pivotal conceptualist and advocate for the new directions called for in the Perkins Act.

the time had come to move away from narrow skills training for specific occupations to broad instruction in "all aspects of the industry."[2]

Just over a century after its founding, Rindge was poised, once again, to play a leading role in defining vocational education. We had a veteran faculty, a new executive director (Larry Rosenstock, a former carpentry teacher at Rindge, returning after two years as a staff attorney for the Center for Law and Education), a new academic coordinator (Adria Steinberg), and the full support of Mary Lou McGrath, the superintendent of the Cambridge Public Schools, who instructed us to comply with the Perkins Act, and to "turn the program upside down and inside out" in order to do so. It was our task to help the faculty put the rhetoric of Perkins and the progressivism of Dewey into daily practice at Rindge.

CityWorks

"Some people seem to have a problem with the Rindge School of Technical Arts. They are always putting RSTA down and stereotyping us: . . . the students in RSTA are dumb; they will not go to college; they are going to drop out. Well, I will not take this anymore! . . . Being a freshman in RSTA, I am positive that I will go to college, and a lot of my confidence has come from my teachers. RSTA students have worked hard, demonstrated enthusiasm, and displayed some great exhibits. We are smart, not only in mind, but also with our hands. We have, or will have shortly, an advanced technological mind as well as an academic mind. . . . We give respect, so we expect respect. Success demands it!"

In March 1993, Paulina Mauras published this statement in our high school newspaper. Her anger is not surprising. As a 9th grader in the vocational wing of Cambridge's comprehensive high school, Paulina suffers from the low status accorded vocational education and all who enter it.

What's worth noting is that this 14-year-old is ready to do something about it. She is acting the way one would hope all members of a participatory democracy could act: speaking out publicly in protest of something she sees as unfair, challenging class stereotypes, showing

---

[2]The Perkins Act mandates that all vocational students "gain strong experience in and understanding of all aspects of the industry they are preparing to enter, including finance, planning, management, underlying principles of technology, technical and production skills, labor issues, community issues, health and safety issues, and environmental issues as they pertain to the industry."

confidence in herself and her working-class peers, and seeing herself as a member of a community.

Paulina's notion of combining hands and mind, and the development of her skills in doing so, come directly from her experiences in City-Works, the centerpiece of the 9th grade program at Rindge. Cambridge is the "text" as students investigate the neighborhoods, the systems, the people, and the needs that compose an urban community. Students work on individual and group projects, bringing aspects of their community into the classroom by creating numerous "artifacts" of Cambridge: maps, photographs, tapes, oral histories, and three-dimensional models.

Several features make this program unusual. First, CityWorks combines key characteristics of vocational programs—a project approach, apprentice-master relationships, and real clients—with the broader content and essential skills of academic education. Projects involve hands-on work, like making a wall-size map of the city and wiring it to light up selected landmarks. At the same time, students engage in problem solving, like deciding where on the map to locate a new teen center that would attract youth from all ethnic and racial communities of the city.

Second, CityWorks is taught in a space designed for collaborative project work. Looking for an alternative to both shops and classrooms, we borrowed the notion of "studios" from design schools. There is an open area at one end of the room for large-group activities such as demonstrations and exhibitions, but most of the room is subdivided into studios where teachers work on projects with small groups of students. This arrangement gives participants the flexibility to regroup, team up, or borrow tools and materials as the project requires.

Third, community representatives are invited to help create a context for students' efforts. Staff members from city agencies and programs identify unmet community needs that students could address and also serve as an authentic audience for students' finished products and presentations.

At a recent exhibition of students' work, several teams of students displayed drawings and scale models of a heritage museum they had designed for Cambridge. Each group had a different conception of where the museum might be located and how it should be designed. The museum builders sat with their models to explain their ideas as parents, city officials, and local businesspeople filtered through the exhibit.

In making the models, the museum builders were responding to a request from the city's tourist agency, which is in the process of raising funds for a museum. Six weeks before the exhibit, the agency director had come to speak to CityWorks students and ask for their help in this effort. With thousands of people visiting the city each year, it was important for students to understand the tourism industry and to help plan its development in a way that would take the needs of residents into account.

In addition to the museum builders, several other groups of students involved themselves in the question of what visitors to the city should see and do. Rejecting existing brochures featuring "Old Cambridge" and Harvard University, one group designed a tour and brochure featuring places of interest to visiting teens, while another created a "Sweet Tour" brochure for visitors seeking the best desserts in town. A third group of students liked the idea of highlighting the efforts of a "local hero." They videotaped an interview with John E. Gittens, a founder of the Cambridge NAACP, and learned that he had led a neighborhood organizing effort to get the city to open a new playground named after a child who was struck by a car when he was playing in the street. Their brochure featured a map locating the playground as well as the story of its creation. All three brochures, along with a T-shirt that another group of CityWorks students designed, have since been adopted by the board of the tourist agency as products that are marketed and distributed.

The goal of CityWorks projects is to help students understand their community and its needs, and ultimately to see themselves as people who can affect that community and create new opportunities for themselves and others who live or work there. Through the lens of community development, students arrive at a very different and more positive vision of what it means to be a vocational student. The point is not just to make things, learn some skills, and get a job, but rather to become thinkers and solvers of problems who work well together in teams and communicate well with various audiences.

Toward Participatory Democracy in School

If Paulina had entered Rindge four years earlier, the program she entered would have been very different from CityWorks, but remarkably similar to the one in place in 1888, when Rindge opened. In fact, thousands of other high schools in this country today still offer such a program: freshmen in vocational education go through an "exploratory" in which they sample each of the shops available in the school, such as metalworking and carpentry. Teachers work in the autonomous isolation of their shops or classrooms; students suffer from low expectations and minimal or diluted academics.

This system, unchanged since its original design for the industrial revolution over a hundred years ago, is based on the outdated and undemocratic premise that 15-year-olds of lower income families should predict their adult occupation (Rosenstock 1991). (Who among us at 15 thought we would be doing what we are doing today?) In short, the 9th grade program functions as the gatekeeping mechanism that begins the stark segregation of vocational students by social class, race, gender, and language ability.

In choosing CityWorks, we rejected the purely consumerist notion of democracy so prevalent in American high schools today, which is that schools offering the most options in courses and shops are best—even if these offerings are shallow and force students into a track. Our goal was to move toward a more participatory model where teachers work together toward the collective interests of the students and the school; where students are engaged, active participants in their learning and in their community; and where parents and community members have real roles in the school's programs. We saw a new mission: to use vocational methods—experiential and contextual learning, team teaching, cooperative learning, and performance assessment—so that vocational students can learn the same basic and advanced academic skills and critical thinking skills that *all* students should learn for further education or for work.

In 1990, more through instinct than anything else, we began a participatory planning process to develop a new 9th grade program. What we didn't realize is that the process of creating CityWorks would be as important in developing a democratic culture as the program itself—because of its impact on teachers.

In embarking on program redesign, we set ourselves three ground rules. The first was to keep everyone in the department informed of all that we were doing. The second was that nobody would have to participate who did not want to. And the third was that those who did not want to participate would not be allowed to interfere with the efforts of those who did. When the first call went out for people to join a design team, six people volunteered.

Letting the Teachers Lead

By the fall of 1991, the team had come up with an overall conceptual framework for CityWorks, fiddled with the schedule to create unprecedented daily meeting time for teachers, and begun to design and renovate a space that would house the new program. We began the school year with enough classroom activities to last only about one month. The rest would have to come from the CityTeam meetings in which everyone teaching the course would participate. Although not having all of City-Works plotted out was a bit terrifying, we knew that handing teachers a finished curriculum would be a mistake.

Teachers, like students, are not empty vessels into which the current wisdom can be poured. For years, vocational teachers at Rindge had spent virtually all of their time at school teaching occupationally specific, narrow, technical skills. Most believed this is what being a vocational teacher was all about. State-mandated curricula reinforced this notion. Vocational teachers received manuals for their shop areas listing duties and tasks that were to fill the students' days.

If we wanted our school to be a place where all kids could be active participants in a democratic culture, we would have to structure a program where all teachers could be too. We would have to encourage teachers to unearth the reasons beneath their current practice, and to reconsider that practice in the light of changing economic and social realities. In other words, we had to respect and make room for them as thinkers as well as doers.

We suspected that Rindge teachers were experiencing a kind of cognitive dissonance. Certainly the curriculum they were teaching at school left out much of what they knew to be important in their own work and lives outside of school. This point was brought home to us early in our reform efforts during a conversation with a teacher who had taught carpentry at Rindge for many years. Like many vocational teachers, he was an independent contractor outside of school. He explained that he would very much like to turn his business over to his sons, both of whom were skilled carpenters. The problem was that neither seemed to be good at most of the other tasks associated with running a successful contracting business: for instance, making good estimates, writing contracts, managing cash flow, dealing with clients and subcontractors, and getting variances from the local zoning board. These are all skills that are rarely taught in vocational schools.

This teacher held within his own experiences the seeds of a new approach to practice. The students in his classes should not be limited to banging nails, but should learn the range of skills that he knew as a parent, citizen, and small contractor were needed by his own sons.[3] The challenge for us has been to create a professional culture that encourages teachers to share their experiences and reflect on their practice. Several strategies have been particularly critical to that effort.

Common Planning Time. The most basic change we have made is to give teachers both informal and formal opportunities to work together. Their close physical proximity in the CityWorks room opens the possibility of joint projects. Daily required CityTeam meetings ensure that such possibilities will be discussed.

To create a meeting time in the daily schedule necessitated closing the shops for a period, an unpopular move with both our own teachers and the counselors from other parts of the high school who signed students up for shops as electives. But the daily meeting time is critical to what we are trying to accomplish. The meetings are a time to reflect on what is happening in CityWorks, to review, revise, and propose curriculum activities and, more generally, to get to know one another and explore the possibilities for collaboration.

Including "Outsiders." From the beginning, the vocational teachers who staffed CityWorks have been joined by a variety of people from very different backgrounds who bring other perspectives and experiences to the task. The "others" have included several academic teachers, a loaned employee from the Polaroid Corporation, bilingual technical assistants, and, as needed, consultants to assist staff—first in their work on curriculum, later on group dynamics and issues of organizational development. Teachers and students must gain experience in and understanding of the new relationships required of them by the world outside of school.

This mixture creates a forum for reexamining assumptions and for moving beyond the specific skills involved in particular trades or subjects to what is important for all students to know and be able to do by the time they leave the program. At one critical junction, for example,

---

[3]"What the best and wisest parent wants for his own child, that must the community want for all of its children." From J. Dewy, *The School and Society* Chicago: University of Chicago Press, 1900), p. 7.

when vocational teachers were resisting collaborative projects in the name of craft specialization, the Polaroid employee talked about the multicraft perspective at his company and at other high-performance workplaces.

Creating Genuine Interdependence. Curricular integration, an end in itself, produces important changes in teacher relationships as well. Once isolated in their own shops, and sometimes competing among themselves for students, teachers now plan curriculum and multidisciplinary projects together. As a result, they are more invested in the whole performance of each student, as well as the performance of the whole school.

The daily teacher meetings are productive because they have to be. All teachers know they are about to go in and teach CityWorks the next day (or the next hour). In a very real sense, they sink or swim together. If the program works, it will eventually increase enrollments and attract a broader clientele of students. If it does not, Rindge will suffer the kinds of staff cutbacks seen in other vocational programs. The competitive ethic of the old exploratory does not die easily, but it really is counterproductive in the new structure. It makes much more sense to collaborate, to nurture and support new ideas, and to look to one another for project ideas and strategies. This shared reflection has contributed to a new level of collegiality at Rindge. Teachers more often talk with one another about teaching. They plan and make instructional materials together, they observe one another, and they are willing to ask for and provide one another with assistance.

Changing Expectations

Changes are evident in both the formal team meetings and informal time that staff spend with one another. During the first few months of CityWorks team meetings, teachers would almost never comment on a teaching or learning issue without prefacing their remarks with a disclaimer: "I would never say what's right for anyone else," or "This is just the way I do things," or "I know that everyone has their own way of doing things and that's fine."

The frequency of such statements provided clues to an underlying group norm that can best be characterized as "noninterference": "I won't look too closely at what you're up to or tell you what to do; and you won't scrutinize me" (Little 1992, p. 49). The isolation of traditional schools and the conditions of teaching make teachers view their work with the sometimes fierce independence of artisans (Huberman 1989). For vocational teachers, this perspective is reinforced by their highly specialized work within the school (and outside) as trade artisans.

In the past, Rindge teachers defended the separateness of their shops by citing the differences among their trades, each with its own specific skill requirements. Shop autonomy seemed a natural, and even necessary, condition of vocational education. The most obvious negative side-effect was the competition for students. But perhaps an even more serious problem was that teachers had no reason to identify, nor any real way to address, the broader educational needs of their students. They focused on finding ways to interest students in specific technical areas, but they did not feel responsible for ensuring that all students become better problem solvers or communicators, or gain a solid base of reading, writing, and quantitative and scientific reasoning skills.

It is impossible to pinpoint a moment when the focus changed, but after two years of team meetings, a sense of broader responsibility is now evident within the group. Teachers now share information and are willing to identify competencies that students need regardless of their schooling or career choices. Staff members routinely team up for multicraft projects, and they sometimes even design classroom projects that do not involve their trade specialty at all.

In the early planning stages for CityWorks, the group tended to swing from cynical skepticism ("This will never work!") to unrealistic enthusiasm ("We're almost done!"). Now teachers approach the task of restructuring with a kind of rolling up of the collective sleeve. We all have a noticeably greater tolerance for ambiguity. People are more willing to bring issues to the team for group problem solving and have found ways to deal constructively with disagreements.

Teachers are also evolving a shared language for talking about how they work together and for getting through the inevitable crises. Perhaps more important, we now have a picture of what we could and should become: a high-performance workplace where staff members are highly interdependent, yet each is an active participant, focusing energy on the tasks at hand.

The amount of time devoted to meetings and the intensity of the staff work have, at times, created a worry that we might become too adult-focused. A school committee member once railed, "I'm sick and tired of hearing about how happy the teachers are at Rindge. What about the kids?" Fortunately, students don't seem to feel this way. When freshmen are asked what is most noticeable or important to them about Rindge, most students begin with this simple statement: "The teachers here really care about you."

Of course, the teachers have always cared about students, but the scope of what they care about has broadened considerably and hence is more evident to the students. In the old way of doing business, teachers had little patience with students who were not ready to make a choice about what they wanted to be and who were not motivated to learn all of the skills of a particular trade. They felt their identity as skilled craftspeople slipping away, to be replaced by a much less desirable identity as "caretakers of marginal students" (Little 1992, p. 26).

CityWorks and the other integrated programs give teachers a new identity. Even if students do not express interest in particular trades, teachers no longer feel like mere caretakers. They know that they can help students develop competencies, interests, and attitudes that will serve them well in future schooling or work. Teachers' feelings of self-efficacy are evident to students. Several freshmen recently surprised a visiting reporter by telling her that what makes Rindge teachers different is that they *like* what they are doing.

Not surprisingly, students respond by becoming more engaged with school; their "creative juices" get going and teachers get to see them at their best. The caring and mutual respect go beyond the classroom walls. For example, during the summer a group of students who had just completed their CityWorks year responded to the invitation from one of their teachers to come up with ways to smooth the entry of incoming freshmen. Using the abbreviation R.S.T.A. (from the Rindge School of Technical Arts), they named themselves "Responsible Students Take Action."

When Paulina and her cohort entered Rindge, they received a new student handbook, covering all of the things the older students wished someone had told them, and they found immediate support in the form of R.S.T.A. student mentors, who had set up a table in the hall to help freshmen with everything from coping with sticky locks on lockers to dealing with hazing.

Impressed by such efforts, staff members have become willing to carve out even more unusual forums for student participation and input. Rindge is probably the only vocational school in America to have its own Innovations Board, with equal membership (and votes) for students and staff. The board was created in late 1991, soon after CityWorks received an Innovations Award from the Ford Foundation. One of ten innovations in state and local government selected nationally from over 1,700 applicants, CityWorks was given $100,000 to "broaden and deepen" the work.

The staff agreed to set aside one-third of this award to be distributed over three years in small grants to other innovations in the Cambridge Schools that would further the CityWorks mission. The process would be overseen by a board with equal representation of students and staff and several slots reserved for community representatives.

At its first few meetings, the board hammered out a mission statement and a set of priorities. Student members were outspoken in these discussions, insisting, for example, that all proposals be submitted by at least one teacher and one student, and that proposals specify the ways in which students would be involved in carrying out the program.

By the spring, board members were reading and evaluating nearly two dozen proposals from all over the school district. After selecting and interviewing the finalists, the board selected nine winners, with proposals ranging from a new student-run radio program to a special summer school for bilingual students. Questioned by teachers and classmates as to why they did not use more of the money internally for Rindge projects and programs, several students spoke passionately of the need to end the isolation of the vocational program. They want the Innovations Fund to encourage teachers and students throughout the school district to try new ways to join hands and minds. Their hope echoes the note sounded by Paulina at the end of her statement to the school: "We give respect, so we expect respect. Success demands it!"

Bringing Change Out in the Open

Educators involved in school reform efforts tend to build a protective wall around what they are doing. If they don't, they believe, they might be accused by parents—or even worse, by school board members—of "experimenting with our children." Although it is possible to work in isolation for a while, the only real protection in the long run lies in convincing key stakeholders of the value, and perhaps the inevitability, of what you are doing.

The changes at Rindge have never been a secret. Staff members and students have made presentations at Parents' Nights, spoken at each of the junior high schools, and hosted hundreds of people at the exhibitions of student work. The interest in CityWorks expressed by the larger community has motivated the staff to make the new program work well and to be able to describe it well to others.

The publicness of what we are doing has caused some local political problems. Speaking for a small but vocal constituency of parents, one school board member accused Rindge of misdirecting working-class students by offering them liberal arts rather than the manual training that they "need." This attack was made through letters to the editor of the local paper, obstruction of even mundane Rindge matters before the school committee, and encouragement of students to leave the district under a state school-choice plan and attend a suburban vocational school. There were requests for state audits in three consecutive years, and one even included an attempt to get the state to decertify our program.

Thus far, such attacks have taken time and energy, but they have also solidified the staff, students, and parents behind the new program. Fortunately, we also receive very positive feedback about what we are doing, both from within the district and around the country. As awareness of the Perkins Act has grown, so have requests to visit our program or to send our teachers out as workshop leaders and presenters. In fact, the requests eventually became so great that we set up our own formal mechanism for handling them: the Hands and Minds Collaborative, funded by the Dewitt Wallace-Readers Digest Foundation and the Mott Foundation, is a joint effort of Rindge and the Center for Law and Education.

Contact with other teachers and other school systems has brought major benefits to our staff. The attitudes, questions, and comments of teachers from other districts become a yardstick against which Rindge teachers can measure the distance they have come, and can reduce the "general physical, social, and educational separation that divorces vocational teachers" from other practitioners (Little 1992, p. 6).

In June 1993, a dozen Rindge teachers served as workshop leaders at a national conference cosponsored by the Center for Law and Education, the Massachusetts Institute of Technology, and the Hands and Minds

Collaborative. It was the job of the workshop leaders to assist the nearly two hundred participants in developing projects that would help them implement the Perkins Act in their own schools. At the last session, after listening to a number of teachers express concerns about the loss of time for trade-specific training, Tom Lividoti, the electrical teacher at Rindge, spoke up: "I used to sound just like that. I was the loudest one complaining about fewer hours in the electrical shop. But what we're doing now brings out creative juices I didn't know kids had; I see developments on the academic end that I never dreamed were possible. I may not be able to turn out second-year apprentice electricians, but I know we are turning out better all-around students."

Academic teachers working with the CityWorks program have also found that they have important messages to share with their colleagues. In spring 1993, Alif Muhammad, the CitySystems teacher, convened a workshop series for Cambridge teachers called "Put the Action Back into Math and Science." Rob Riordan, a member of the Rindge Humanities team, addressed humanities teachers and scholars recently at a national meeting sponsored by the American Council of Learned Societies: "I started the year thinking it was my mission to bring humanities into vocational education. Now I believe we must bring vocational methodologies into the humanities."

Dilemmas and Challenges Remain

When we began to re-create ourselves, we knew that we wanted the school to be democratic in all of its many layers. The relations between administration and staff would be as egalitarian as possible and teachers would enjoy meaningful participation in decision making. The relations between teachers would be democratic: there would be opportunities for teachers to diversify their roles, to team teach, and to have regular common planning time. The relations between teachers and students would be democratic: the teacher would act as coach and advisor rather than as a distant lecturer.

The methodology and curriculum would be democratic: we would not track, and therefore we would have the same high expectations for all students. We would focus our assessment on student-originated projects, not teacher-designed tests. The relationship between the school and the community would be democratic: it would afford opportunities for students to investigate and actively seek to meet real community needs.

Finally, we would also try to make our physical environment—our work spaces—as democratic as possible: we would design and build spaces that further our democratic goals, despite the typical American high school architecture, which reflects the industrial factory model and "gets in the way" of collective work.[4]

But the fundamental conundrum of vocational education remains insufficiently resolved: many still want from vocational education the "no-frills" schooling that they view as suitable for lower income students, while others of us agree with Dewey that it is a vehicle for transforming secondary education and creating schools where all students can be "smart."

One of the most troubling aspects of our experience at Rindge is the persistent social-class bias that pervades certain community members' beliefs about who should attend vocational programs and what they should be doing once they are there. One critic noted that the new Rindge is preparing "Renaissance people, not plumbers." It goes without saying which he preferred for his own daughters, yet he still insisted narrow skills were better for low-income students.

This bias has its roots in the contradictory origins of our school, and it will not fall easily in Cambridge—or elsewhere. Even Dewey, in commenting on this bias, noted with an aggravated sarcasm, "Nothing in the history of education is more touching than to hear some successful leaders denounce as undemocratic the attempt to give all the children at public expense the fuller education which their own children enjoy as a matter of course" (Westbrook 1991, p. 178). At its core, this is what the experiment at Rindge seeks to achieve: to counter the reduction of education to job training (Davis et al. 1989, p. 109) that only "erects more barriers to high-quality education for low-income students" (Rosenstock 1992), and to broaden creative intellectual work for all students.

---

[4]Assembly line architecture is supported by assembly line methodologies and curricula. See A. Steinberg, "Beyond the Assembly Line," *The Harvard Education Letter* 9, 2 (1993): 1.

References

Carnoy, M., and H. Levin. (1985). *Schooling and Work in the Democratic State.* Stanford, Calif.: Stanford University Press.

Davis, J., J. Huot, N. Jackson, R. Johnston, D. Little, G. Martell, P. Moss, D. Noble, J. Turk, and G. Wilson. (1989). *It's Our Own Knowledge.* Toronto: Ontario Federation of Labor Conference on Education and Training.

Dewey, J. (In press). "Some Dangers in the Present Movement for Industrial Education." In *The Middle Works: 1899–1924,* edited by Jo Ann Boydston. Carbondale: Southern Illinois University Press.

Krug, E. (1969). *The Shaping of the American High School, 1880–1920.* Madison: University of Wisconsin Press.

Little, J.W. (1992). "Work on the Margins: The Experience of Vocational Teachers in Comprehensive High Schools." Berkeley: National Center for Research in Vocational Education.

National Assessment of Vocational Education. (1987) Washington, D.C.: United States Department of Education.

Rosenstock, L. (1991). "The Walls Come Down: The Overdue Reunification of Vocational and Academic Education." *Phi Delta Kappan* 72, 6: 434–436.

Rosenstock, L. (December 10, 1992). "Easing Students' Pressure to Predict the Future" [Letter to the editor]. *New York Times,* p. 20.

Westbrook, R. (1991). *John Dewey and American Democracy.* Ithaca, N.Y.: Cornell University Press.

4

La Escuela Fratney:
A Journey Toward Democracy

BOB PETERSON

It was to have been a fairly typical student role play followed by group discussion, an activity students were used to participating in. But, as often happens, my 5th graders surprised me. As Gilberto, Juan, and Carlos took the stage, I knew only that they would be dramatizing some form of discrimination, the topic of today's lesson. The other students and I were astounded when we realized that Gilberto and Juan were acting the part of two gay men trying to rent an apartment from Carlos, the landlord who refused to rent to them.

I was surprised in part because in previous brainstorming sessions on discrimination, nobody had mentioned discrimination against homosexuals. Further, my students had already shown they were apt to uncritically accept anti-gay slurs and stereotypes. But here were Gilberto, Juan, and Carlos, on their own initiative, transferring our discussion of discrimination based on race to discrimination based on sexual preference.

The role play caused an initial chorus of laughs and catcalls, but students then listened attentively to the presentation. Afterward, I asked the class what type of discrimination had been modeled.

"Gayism!" one student yelled out.

It was a new word, but it got the point across. The class went on to discuss "gayism." Most of the kids who spoke agreed that it was a form of discrimination. During the discussion, one student mentioned a march on Washington a week earlier that people had organized to demand gay rights (Gilberto, Juan, and Carlos said they were unaware of the march).

Elvis, who coined the term gayism, then said: "Yeah, my cousin is one of those lesi . . . lesi . . . "

"Lesbians," I said, completing his sentence.

"Yeah, lesbians," he said. He then added enthusiastically, "And she went to Washington to march for her rights."

"That's just like when Dr. King made his dream speech at the march in Washington," another student added.

Before long, the class moved on to a new role play. But the dramatization lingered in my memory. I was proud that the class had been able to move beyond our typical discussions of gay issues, which had seemed to center on my explaining why students shouldn't call each other "faggot." More fundamentally, however, the incident reminded me of the inherent links between classroom and society: how society influences the children who show up in our classrooms for six hours a day and how broader movements for social reform affect daily classroom life.

Some might think it unusual for 5th graders to dramatize discrimination against homosexuals. But then, many things about La Escuela Fratney may surprise those used to more traditional forms of schooling.

The Struggle to Establish La Escuela Fratney

Forged in a battle with a recalcitrant school administration, La Escuela Fratney in Milwaukee, Wisconsin, is the site of a continuing journey to create a school governed by parents and teachers. We describe ourselves as a two-way bilingual, multicultural, whole language school governed by a site-based council. The school currently has 360 students in 4-year-old kindergarten through 5th grade, of whom 65 percent are Hispanic; 20 percent, African American; 13 percent, white; and the remainder, Asian and Native American. Nearly 70 percent of students are eligible for free lunches. We have a Learning Disabilities program conducted primarily through team teaching, and we have a separate program for three- to five-year-olds with exceptional needs.

At each new leg of our journey, we have encountered significant problems that reflect how our society, despite its democratic rhetoric, is in many ways undemocratic. Among the problems: a central office wedded to autocratic methods of leadership, a school system structured to inhibit collaborative teaching practices, parents and teachers tied to the authoritarian habits of their own schooling, students conditioned by a mass-media culture that values individual consumption over the common good, and a socioeconomic system that places little value on urban schools and the families served by them.

In this chapter, you'll learn how a group of committed teachers and parents dealt with these problems. You'll find out how the school attempts to meaningfully involve all parents, not just the most educated and articulate, in the work of the school. And you'll see how the school attempts to uphold its democratic ideals, despite pressures ranging from budget cuts to drugs and violence.

Political Battles

The 90-year-old Fratney Street School was marked for demolition. In April 1988, the staff and students of the school were to move to a new building six blocks away. That the neighborhood around Fratney was one of the few racially integrated, working-class neighborhoods in the city meant little to the school bureaucracy. Some people, however, had a vision of Fratney as the home of an educational program that capitalized on the unique features of the neighborhood. As one parent said, "We started to dream about a school that would provide the highest quality education for all of our children, black, white, and Hispanic."

On January 1, 1988, this small group of teachers, parents, and community activists made their vision public by issuing a press release under the name Neighbors for a New Fratney. The press release called on the Milwaukee School Board to support our proposal to create a whole language, two-way bilingual, multicultural, site-based-managed school at the Fratney School site. We called this new school La Escuela Fratney.

School administrators, however, wanted to turn the building into a new school, an Exemplary Teaching Center staffed by master teachers using the techniques of Madeline Hunter. District teachers having classroom difficulties would then come to the center for $2\frac{1}{2}$-week training sessions, working with "master" teachers in their classrooms. Many parents questioned whether kids should be taught by a series of bad teachers. They also argued that a teaching center could be established anywhere, while the success of La Escuela Fratney depended on its being in one of the few multiracial neighborhoods in Milwaukee.

Neighbors for a New Fratney (NNF) held community meetings and mobilized for a key public hearing. The hearing coincided with a bitter snowstorm that forced all schools to close the next day. Still, the turnout for the meeting was so large that it convinced school board members of the need to give NNF's proposal serious consideration. They directed school administrators to meet with our group and come back with a revised recommendation.

From the beginning, the leaders at the central office did not appear to understand NNF's proposal. Although they issued a compromise proposal that they said combined their teacher training program with our project, many features of our proposal were the antithesis of theirs. For example, a central point of our proposal was that the school would be run by a site-based council of parents and teachers; the administrators wanted a teacher training school organized and run by the central office. As we negotiated with the top administrators in the superintendent's conference room, the absurdity of the situation became evident. I pointed out to then-superintendent Hawthorne Faison that there was an inherent contradiction between a school run by a staff development academy and a school run by a local group of teachers and parents. The central office's proposal for the Exemplary Teacher Center did not even mention parents.

"Wait!" responded one top administrative official. "While it's true we didn't mention parents once in our proposal, your proposal didn't mention central office."

We stuck to our position and continued to mobilize the community. Several developments gave us additional momentum. A few months earlier, the school board had publicly gone on record in favor of site-based management. School board members had also become aware of the benefits of a whole language teaching approach, in part due to the efforts of *Rethinking Schools,* a quarterly newspaper published in Milwaukee whose editorial board included two members of NNF (Peterson 1987, 1988; Tenorio 1986, 1988). And members of the African American community, led by Howard Fuller (our current superintendent), were demanding an independent school district, charging among other things that the bureaucracy was incapable of listening to African American parents.

The long and short of it was that the school board passed the proposal and established the first citywide specialty school to give enrollment preference to children living in the school's immediate neighborhood. The board also directed the central office to cooperate with NNF.

One additional factor seemed to enter into the board's decision, at least for one member. A few months after the vote, this member confessed to me that his approval of La Escuela Fratney was strongly influenced by the quality of the teaching his son was receiving in the 1st grade classroom of a whole language teacher. During a key school board meeting, he said, he found himself during a break discussing the Fratney proposal with a top administrator and realized that the man hadn't the slightest idea of what the proposal involved. "Quite honestly," the board member told me, "I didn't really know what you were talking about either, but I knew this much: My son had started 1st grade in the classroom of a teacher who used what she called whole language techniques. By Thanksgiving, my kid was coming home and writing and publishing his own books, excited about reading and writing, loving to read and to be read to. I knew I had to support your proposal."

The school board's approval essentially concluded the first stage of our struggle, the struggle for political power. It had lasted eight weeks.

Administrative Battles

During the second stage, we confronted the basic tasks involved in developing the program: renovating the facility, selecting the principal and other staff, putting in place the curriculum and related materials. Unfortunately, what the administration failed to do politically at the board level, they tried to do administratively.

For example, despite the school board's explicit order that the central office should cooperate with NNF, two weeks passed with no meeting or contact between the two groups. Finally, we heard through a friend at central office that an important meeting to plan the new Fratney was to take place the next day, a Friday, at 11:00 a.m. Uninvited, the NNF members decided to launch a surprise attack on the central office by sending a parent representative to this meeting. Our plan was to have her arrive a few minutes after the scheduled starting time and then ask a secretary for directions to the meeting. We hoped the secretary would simply assume the parent was supposed to be at the meeting and point her to the proper conference room. Our plan worked: the secretary escorted the parent into a room of open-mouthed administrators. At that time, a joint meeting was set up to start the planning.

For the next several months, from March through September, administrators placed one obstacle after another in the way of constructing the new program. We also had to contend with the typical bureaucratic procedures of a 100,000-student school system, which were not designed to effectively support any sort of grass-roots initiative. These problems were compounded because few members of NNF had the time or expertise to navigate the administrative bureaucracy; most of our volunteers worked on the Fratney project after putting in a full day of work. Our recommendations were often ignored or approved only late in the process.

For example, to deal with union seniority rules that might allow teachers to transfer to Fratney even though they disagreed with the program's approach, NNF proposed that announcements of staff openings be accompanied by a one-page explanation of the school's program. The Milwaukee Teachers Education Association agreed, as did lower level administrators. But the higher authorities decided against this strategy.

NNF called for a nationwide search for a principal. The administration refused, and then proceeded to stall in hiring anyone. Finally, a month before school was to open, and in opposition to what a parent committee had recommended, the administration recommended the appointment of a woman whose experience was limited to suburban schools. She was bilingual, but in English and German, not English and Spanish. NNF viewed this action as a direct affront to the community, and once again the community mobilized. Dozens of parents came to school board meetings, many of them waving picket signs. Bowing to pressure and publicity, newly hired Superintendent Robert S. Peterkin (from Cambridge, Massachusetts) recognized the problem and rejected the recommendation. Peterkin hired an interim principal acceptable to the community.

Developing the curriculum posed additional problems. In late June and July, three teachers settled in at the central office building to write a draft curriculum. Resources for the teachers seemed almost nonexistent: the teachers were given information only in response to specific questions, and secretarial help seemed in extremely short supply. One of the teachers remarked that working on the Fratney project at the central office was like being a peace activist in the Pentagon.

The stonewalling continued. For example, despite repeated requests, the administrator in charge of ordering furniture refused to exchange the school's old "bicycle desks" (chairs attached to desks) for separate desks and chairs, which are more conducive to cooperative grouping. One day, a member of NNF told the administrator that we had changed our minds: we wanted the old desks to stay because on the first day of school, parents, teachers, and students were going to pile them on the playground and then call a press conference to expose the administration for failing to support our project. The next morning, two truckloads of new desks were delivered to the school.

When the new staff arrived in mid-August to make what we thought were to be final preparations for an opening a few weeks later, we found that necessary renovation had only begun and that the school had not been cleaned since the spring. Curiously, nothing we had ordered in July had yet arrived. We called vendors, and they told us they had no record of our orders. Much to our horror, we discovered that although the requisition forms had been signed on July 18th or earlier by an associate superintendent, the forms had sat in the purchasing division for a month because the department did not have an authorization card with the associate superintendent's signature. The missing materials were a serious problem; many books had disappeared when the school closed, the two-way bilingual program required new materials, and the few remaining library books were in boxes because of the delayed renovation of the library. We would have to start school with virtually no materials. "Well, at least we ordered a high-quality Xerox machine," one teacher said hopefully. "We can rely on that for the first few weeks of school." But, of course, a phone call confirmed that this order, too, had somehow been lost.

We stormed into the central office building. Fortunately, this time we had two allies: Superintendent Peterkin and his assistant, Deborah McGriff, who was flabbergasted by our story. She listened intently as we hinted that our next step would be around-the-clock occupation of the school. She took immediate steps to get the administrators in line. A photocopy machine appeared in the school the next day. Materials were shipped via airmail. At a meeting the next day, the administrators who had put up road blocks were now at our beck and call.

After visiting La Escuela Fratney on the first day of school, Super-intendent Peterkin called Fratney a model of his version of school reform, referring specifically to the value of extensive parental involvement and a unified vision of what a school should be. Finally, the tide had turned.

Key Components of the Fratney Program

Starting a new school with several important components was an immense challenge, even with the high level of energy coming off the successful struggle to establish the school. In theory, the components fit well together, but in daily classroom life, each took a big effort to get going well. We consider each to be an integral part of our school's vision.

Two-Way Bilingual Program

An important component of the Fratney program is our commitment to a two-way bilingual program in which native Spanish and English speakers are in the same classrooms, with children receiving half their instruction in English and half in Spanish. This arrangement avoids separating children by language dominance and gives meaning and purpose to the acquisition of two languages.

The belief anchoring this approach is that all children have the right to learn two languages, including their native language. By consciously striving to create equality between the languages in our building, we are modeling a broad concept of equality for our children. Given the intimate link between culture and language, instruction in two languages also promotes multicultural understanding. And a two-way bilingual approach enhances students' self-esteem, because students soon learn that no matter what social class they come from, they bring something of value to the classroom: their language.

Two-way bilingual programs in the United States, however, have numerous problems (Edelsky 1991), primarily stemming from the politically subordinate role any second language necessarily has in this country. Fratney's program is no exception. We have learned that successful bilingual learning requires a strict separation of the two languages and language environments, so children are forced to use their second language and teachers are encouraged to stay in the target language. If classes are always conducted bilingually (i.e., a teacher explains the material first in one language and then another), students may rely on their native tongue.

By the end of our second year, we realized that English was still too dominant in our school. We looked at the experience of two-way bilingual schools in other cities and critically examined our practices. Discussions were held among staff, at a site-based council meeting, and at a special meeting of parents of students in the two kindergarten classrooms where the method for bilingual instruction differed from that used in the rest of the school. At the beginning of our third year, we adopted for the whole school the instructional method used in these kindergartens: Two teachers of the same grade team-teach between 54 and 60 children in two groups of 27 to 30 children per class. One day, they go to the Spanish room and receive instruction in Spanish; the next day, they go to the English room and receive instruction in English. The teachers are bilingual, but one teaches in English and one in Spanish. This approach has increased the use of Spanish in our school and encouraged team teaching. At the same time, it has exacerbated the problem of lack of common planning time and complicated other matters such as assessment, report cards, and parent-teacher conferences. In our seventh year of operation, the 4th and 5th grade teachers addressed these problems by alternating classes every two calendar weeks instead of every other day. This arrangement allows for more consistent instruction and more timely completion of student projects.

Although Fratney's program has clearly been successfully in helping students with limited English proficiency learn English while maintaining their Spanish, it has been less successful in helping native English speakers learn Spanish. The staff and parents are trying to address this problem through peer observation, research of other schools that may be more successful, and a comparative analysis of the English-dominant students who excel in the program and those who don t.

Despite these problems, the two-way bilingual program is one of Fratney's strengths. It sends a strong message to students and their families about the equivalent value of Spanish and English and the people who speak these languages. Because Spanish-speaking parents know the school values their language, they feel more comfortable in visiting and volunteering at our school. The bilingual program has sent a signal to the larger Latino community that staff and parents of La Escuela Fratney are strongly committed to broader issues of equality.

Multicultural, Antiracist Curriculum

Our vision of multiculturalism goes beyond what we call "the three F's": facts, foods, and faces. Although our classes include projects that focus on human relations, they also include lessons on race and power. We highlight the experiences of people of color in our schoolwide themes, and we attempt to draw on music, history, art, stories, poetry, and literature from various geopolitical groups, such as African Americans, Hispanics, Native Americans, and Asian Americans. We also teach our students to be antiracist; we teach that racism is unscientific and immoral, that it has been a damaging social disease throughout U.S. history. Teachers are encouraged to teach about stereotypes, prejudice, and all forms of discrimination.

Given the diversity of our student and family population, such a multicultural, antiracist policy is important not only for our long-range educational goals but also for our immediate survival as a community of learners.

The success of this curriculum has been uneven. Some of the more outspoken white, middle-class parents complained that our school was teaching only minority history and shortchanging students of European heritage. Others complained that their kids weren't learning the national anthem and the pledge of allegiance. Some teachers felt that such criticism, if left unchecked, would push Fratney back into the mainstream, where curricular content might talk of democracy, but violate what many consider one of the fundamental building blocks of democracy—the equality of all people—in its continued emphasis on European points of view.

At times, such issues exploded at meetings. For example, at one site-based council meeting, a white parent questioned the absence of the pledge of allegiance in the classroom, and a young Puerto Rican teacher responded by describing how angry she became every time she had to recite the pledge of allegiance, because it reminded her that Puerto Rico has endured decades of U.S. colonial rule without "liberty and justice for all." The parent said she had never realized anyone at the school might have felt that way.

Such differences of opinion don't go away. And the absence of such controversy at a school doesn't mean differences don't exist; it's more likely that people are just mirroring our society's propensity to remain silent on the sensitive issue of race. A school that wants to foster a healthy multicultural atmosphere should be committed to sustaining an ongoing conversation about matters of race and culture in such a way that all voices are present and dominant modes of thought are challenged.

One of Fratney's strategies for encouraging the expression of diverse points of view was to develop a year-long process in which the staff and parents defined what we meant by multicultural, antiracist education. Working through the parent curriculum committee, the site-based management council, and staff meetings, parents and staff went through five drafts to come up with a joint statement that outlines the philosophy and implementation of multicultural, antiracist education at La Escuela Fratney.

The statement is a good starting point, and helps orient new staff and parents. But no document can capture the learning process that was the year-long debate itself. Thus, we have sought to find additional ways to sustain the conversation and increase our understanding of how to teach multiculturally.

We have also found it useful to define multicultural, antiracist education on a continuum, as described by educators James Banks (1991) and Enid Lee (Miner 1991). Such a framework is helpful in giving teachers a reasonable way to view their growth in this area. The continuum begins with teachers just talking about the contributions of people of color, then adding material to the existing curriculum. It moves to thoroughly integrating instruction on non-European cultures into many subject areas. Finally, it develops to a more transformative and active stage where students and teachers critique the messages they get from television, children's books, and textbooks. The ultimate goal is that students and teachers not only understand the world, but engage in social action to change it.

Even with the school policy statement and the continuum, we discovered some problems. First, there were unnecessary duplications and omissions in what was covered. For example, a student going from kindergarten through 5th grade studied little Asian American history and too much African American history focused on Harriet Tubman and Martin Luther King Jr. Second, as new staff came to the school, they needed more specificity than either the policy statement or continuum provided.

Using another process that involved staff inservice and discussions at site-based management meetings, we came up with a document that lays out a framework for which geopolitical groups should (at a minimum) be emphasized at which grade level, thus ensuring that students are exposed to the history and culture of each major group at least twice during their years at Fratney.

Whole Language and Natural Second Language Learning

We believe children learn to listen, speak, read, and write by listening, speaking, reading, and writing. Our classrooms aim to be student-centered, experience-based, and language-rich. What does this mean? All of our students write in journals daily. We use big books, shared reading, book clubs, story telling, the writing process, interactive journals, drama, and puppetry. Many classrooms publish books written by our students, and the books are then cataloged and shelved in our school library.

A fundamental reason for this approach to language arts instruction is our belief that education should be based on the experience of the children, and be relevant to their lives, families, and communities. By thinking, investigating, and writing about our community, children reconfirm their own and their families' worth and simultaneously gain knowledge about the problems that they and our society as a whole must confront. Many teachers use homework assignments that encourage children to survey their community and interview family members and neighbors. This activity validates the importance of what the average person thinks and also forges stronger ties between family, school, and community.

Our approach to language arts instruction has led to considerable debate and discussion in the Fratney community. Even though parents must volunteer to send their children to Fratney, many do so unaware of the school's particular instructional philosophy, which occasionally creates problems. Some parents find the teaching methods foreign because they are unlike those they experienced. Others are critical because they fear that when their kids enter the real world they will have to be familiar with textbooks, spelling tests, and standardized tests.

The issue of how to teach spelling has perhaps occupied as much time at our curricular meetings as any other topic. There has been no easy way to resolve the conflicting opinions on this subject, basically because there is no surefire way to teach spelling. We have conducted numerous workshops and discussions on spelling and whole language, stressing that the key to successful language learning is involvement in meaningful reading and writing experiences. At the same time, we cannot escape the political pressures that come with the annual publishing of test scores in the local paper and have adapted to these by ensuring that we teach test-taking skills as a life-survival skill.

Cooperative Learning and Discipline

Cooperative learning and classroom management come up in almost any discussion of democracy in schools. The first year of the Fratney program verged on disaster because we overestimated the responsibilities our students would be able to handle. Specifically, we failed to anticipate that a large percentage of the children who chose to come to our school were having little success at their previous school. Many students lacked basic self-management skills. They were unable to handle rights as simple as being able to take a pass and go to the bathroom on their own (i.e., without direct teacher permission). We realized that we had to consciously help students make the transition from the past, where they had been treated like mindless sheep, to the future, where we wanted them to act like responsible human beings.

During our second year, we wrote a Chapter I proposal that put a self-esteem specialist in our school full-time. She team-taught with classroom teachers, using specific interventions to enhance students' self-esteem. We also built a peer mediation program involving 4th and 5th graders, which has met with moderate success. We do considerable cross-age tutoring, with older children helping the younger ones as they read and write books together. This kind of tutoring helps both groups of students. For example, a 4th grade teacher was having trouble with her students' behavior when they went on walking field trips to the nearby Milwaukee River. The kids would get too close to certain parts of the river. This behavior changed dramatically when she paired her students with 1st graders. The older students outdid themselves to make sure that the younger students didn't go too near the water.

Our teachers also use class meetings, not only to help set classroom rules at the beginning of each year but to solve problems throughout the year, and to plan each class's approach to our schoolwide themes.

Many of our teachers use a cooperative management approach that involves dividing the class into groups. For example, I arrange the desks in my classroom in five groups of six desks, each of which is a base group. Every group has its own bookshelf where materials are stored and homework is turned in. Each group elects a captain, who makes sure materials are in order and group members are paying attention and participating in activities.

I divide students into mixed groups every nine weeks, taking into account language dominance, race, gender, and special needs. Throughout the day, students may work in a variety of other cooperative learning configurations, but their base group remains the same. The base group arrangement allows students to take on many of the classroom management tasks, which helps them develop a sense of responsibility for the functioning of the class. This arrangement also provides positive peer pressure that helps kids work better in the classroom.

Nonetheless, discipline problems persist, sometimes chronic ones. These problems require both long-term curricular planning, such as teaching children "I messages" and setting up peer mediation programs, and short-term intervention strategies. Our culture does a great job of teaching children to be disrespectful of people on the basis of a host of attributes. While our multicultural curriculum addresses this problem throughout students' years at Fratney, teachers must act decisively to improve students' immediate behavior. Maggie Melvin, the school librarian, talked about how teachers deal with disruptions and put-downs when she told *Teaching Tolerance* magazine that "So often, when we're in the middle of an incident, we want to fix-it, make everything OK, and go on with the lesson. But here [at Fratney], we try to make sure that when you're in the middle of the incident, it gets processed. . . . Those are the truly teachable moments in terms of human relations, and if you believe that's an important lifetime skill, you stop the lesson and deal with it" (Ahlgren 1993, p. 30).

A Thematic Curriculum Approach

We try to integrate as much of the curriculum as possible through schoolwide themes, which teachers and parents develop annually. Our themes generally stress social responsibility and action, as these examples illustrate: "We Respect Ourselves and the World," "We Send Messages When We Communicate," "We Can Make a Difference on Planet Earth," and "We Tell Stories of the World." Within the context of each theme, we also try to choose a schoolwide project. For example, in exploring the theme "We Send Messages When We Communicate," students studied the subtheme "TV Can Be Dangerous to Your Health."

We organized a "No-TV Week" during which students, their families, and staff pledged not to watch television for an entire week.

During the theme "We Can Make a Difference on Planet Earth," each class chose a project that they thought would show they could make a difference. The nine-week theme culminated in a project show that allowed students to share what they had done. Projects included recycling, raising money for homeless children in El Salvador, treating one another better in the classroom, and testifying at a public hearing in favor of creating a nature preserve adjacent to the Milwaukee River.

Our use of schoolwide themes has helped teachers new to Fratney more quickly understand some of our underlying philosophies and methods. It has also helped bring students and staff together to work on projects, underscoring those things that we have in common.

Critical Thinking

In a society whose mass culture exhibits numerous antidemocratic tendencies ranging from political apathy to institutionalized racist and sexist practices, engendering democratic sentiments within children is a challenge. At Fratney, we have a commitment to encouraging children to think deeply about the world and to helping them develop their ability to critique society and their role within it.

The "No-TV Week" project mentioned earlier is one of our strategies for raising such issues. The first year we conducted this campaign, about half the students, parents, and teachers pledged not to watch any television for a week. In discussions following that week without television, the parent curriculum committee and the site-based management council met to discuss the experiment. They concluded that although not watching TV for a week might help some students permanently alter their viewing habits, the school really needed to consider how to teach children to view media critically, because the reality is that most children will continue to watch lots of television.

Recognizing the validity of these criticisms, teachers focused more the next year on helping students develop critical thinking skills that they can use as they watch TV shows and read advertisements. For example, a 2nd grade teacher had her class make huge murals out of clipped magazine advertisements so students could examine what kinds of people were held up as models in our society. They found racial bias, gender stereotypes, and an almost complete absence of heavy people and people with glasses. A group of teachers also used videotapes of the TV show *Teenage Mutant Ninja Turtles* and accompanying advertisements to help students examine violence on television.

Each year the site-based management council decides whether we should repeat "No-TV Week" that year and discusses possible changes in the project. We also confront difficult questions: How can we control an activity that, according to the American Academy of Pediatrics, consumes more time than any other childhood activity except sleeping? How can we counter an activity that fosters mental and physical passivity and undermines creativity? That perpetuates sexual and racial stereotypes, promotes violence, and encourages the buying of useless or expensive products and unhealthy food? That presents a distorted view of reality? How can we encourage family activities that are alternatives to TV and video game addictions, but are sensitive to the pressures of many single-parent households?

Many successes are recounted during such discussions. One parent, for example, explained that before "No-TV Week," her family always watched TV during dinner; after the week without TV, she told the children that the television would be banned during dinner so that family members could talk to each other.

Another parent decided to institute no-TV days three or four times a week. Another put the family's television in an attic room to discourage TV viewing. A fourth said her two children now ask for a no-TV night so they can play games with mom and dad.

Despite differing opinions on how best to deal with the many problems such a project engenders, the Fratney staff and parents continue to support the effort, albeit with modifications to help enhance participation. Each year students and adults sign no-TV contracts, keep logs of their television viewing habits, write diaries of how they survived a "No-TV Week," interview family members about the impact of television on their lives, and examine stereotypes and advertisements on TV.

Governance

Since its inception, Fratney has been committed to governance of the school by the teachers and parents who are the main actors at the school. This decision has not been without conflict. For example, differences emerged over the composition of the council that would run the school. In the months before the school opened, the steering committee of NNF was essentially making all decisions for the school. Power had to be transferred from this group to the teachers who would work there and to the parents whose children had enrolled. One member of the steering committee suggested the council include two parents elected from each of the 11 classrooms and only two teacher representatives; another suggested that the council have equal parent and teacher representation. The matter was partially resolved when we learned of a new agreement between the school board and the teachers union prescribing that all such councils need teacher representation totaling 50 percent plus one teacher. After much discussion, NNF decided that fighting the school board and teachers union would be futile; instead, we decided to adhere to the agreement, but include in our council's procedures a provision for parent alternates that would essentially ensure equal voice at site-based council meetings.

The site-based management council of parents and staff members meets monthly and makes all major decisions concerning the school. We chose our principal; rewrote our report card; developed polices regarding homework, parent involvement, and multicultural education; redirected parts of our school budget; and developed a policy that encouraged critical discussion of current events, such as the Persian Gulf War. We also have a curriculum committee, a fund-raising committee, and a building committee, the latter being a group of staff that meets regularly to deal with immediate school issues. For example, the building committee has dealt with how to provide schoolwide support for struggling new teachers and how to reapportion assignments for educational assistants among classrooms when one assistant is out due to long-term illness.

Significant Parent Involvement

Significant parent involvement is part of almost every successful school. Many parents were significantly involved in our struggle to establish La Escuela Fratney and develop its curriculum. Once the school opened, however, the initial euphoria diminished and parent involvement declined. The parents who remained active were mostly white and middle-class, even though white children make up a small percentage of our students.

We did three things to try to counter this imbalance and foster broader parental involvement. First, we established quotas for our site-based management council, so that African American and Latino parents were ensured seats. Second, we decided to redirect money from our budget to hire two part-time parent organizers, a Mexican American and an African American. Eventually, these two part-time positions became one full-time position. Finally, with the help of the Wisconsin Writing Project, which is part of the National Writing Project, we developed a parent project. We paid 15 parents to participate in a six-week evening workshop in which they discussed school issues and wrote about their children. Parents who didn't usually participate in school activities were encouraged to participate. Several parents in the workshop have decided to remain active in other aspects of our school.

Tension between parents was sometimes a problem. For instance, middle-class white parents clashed with single mothers of African American or Latino heritage. As Christine Bowditch (1993) points out, "The rhetoric of parent involvement, at least in many of its manifestations, assumes, legitimates, and seeks to enforce a particular normative model of the family—a model . . . that has become decreasingly representative of American families across socioeconomic classes." At Fratney, this problem sometimes could be seen in the tendency of some middle-class parents to judge a parent's commitment to the school by the number of meetings the parent was willing to attend. These parents became "meeting happy," wanting to schedule frequent meetings at which they worked long hours. The logistics and expense of child care were not even an issue in their lives.

We have sought to overcome this problem by ensuring that meeting agendas are well planned, meetings are well run, and much of the actual work is done in smaller subcommittees at times and places convenient to the parents. For example, in conjunction with a neighborhood-based community group, our site-based council has launched a new parent group called the Friends of Fratney. The group meets monthly for breakfast immediately after the school day begins, a time that is convenient for many single mothers who drop off their children (as long as other siblings are welcome to attend).

Links to Community

La Escuela Fratney is committed to community involvement because we realize that the lives of staff, students, and parents extend beyond the school, and that the broader community in turn directly affects our students.

In our third year, for instance, we worked with community activists to get a new a playground for young children at our school. Our tot lot was dominated by a jungle gym in the shape of a tank. When we took over the school, we refused to follow the easy route to have it removed, as some in the peace movement recommended. Instead, we involved parents and students in the process and set our goal in the larger context of peace education.

Our preparation paid off when we requested that the city give us $70,000 to get a new tot lot. The mayor's office initially opposed our request, saying the city replaced only two tot lots a year, and we were number 60 on the list. The thought of waiting 30 years didn't hold much appeal for us. Their second argument was that if they gave in to the Fratney parents and students, then other school communities would demand the same. That's exactly what should happen, we said, as we proceeded with our organizing and won the new tot lot.

Another community project involved the closing of a tavern across the street from our playground. The littering of school property and the tavern's overall negative influence on the neighborhood convinced the site-based management council and other parents and teachers to lobby and get the tavern's liquor license revoked.

The school is currently working with local community-based organizations to plan a program and secure funding to expand our after-school program to better serve our students and the neighborhood kids who attend other schools.

What Have We Learned?

Annual budget battles have taken a toll on the Fratney project. During the last two months of each school year, we had hoped to be able to reflect on our progress and devise improvements for the following year. Instead, for three consecutive years staff and parents spent hundred of hours in communitywide efforts to prevent budget cutbacks that would have qualitatively damaged our program. Although we have so far been successful in holding off fatal cutbacks, the energies and time expended in these efforts have significantly stalled our efforts to improve Fratney's program.

Our commitment to site-based management has led many teachers and parents to sometimes feel swallowed up by the life of the school. Naturally, the running of the school is our top priority, but we have also felt the need to be involved in changing policies at the district level that would directly improve conditions at Fratney. Many teachers, for instance, not only fulfill their classroom duties, but also participate in the work of textbook adoption committees (Peterson 1989); citywide teacher councils that deal with whole language instruction and multicultural curriculum; the district library council; and various task forces and commissions, especially those concerning districtwide curriculum reform (Levine 1991).

Many of the expectations we had at the beginning of this project have been turned on their head. Few people thought that approval of this neighborhood school was a real possibility; even fewer imagined the magnitude of realizing our vision, should the proposal be approved. The process of bringing La Escuela Fratney into being has been a difficult but rewarding one that has taught us many lessons.

Lesson 1: Grass-roots movements can produce real change.

An important lesson from the initial stage of our struggle is best summed up in the words of Margaret Mead: "Never doubt that a small group of thoughtful committed citizens can change the world; indeed it's the only thing that ever has." Both the progressive political community and the educational community in Milwaukee were shocked at our initial victory. People have become so accustomed to losing social struggles that a clear victory was unexpected. When people asked, "How did you do it?" the simple response was "Hard work, being well organized, and acting quickly when opportunities presented themselves." Teachers and parents, having been inculcated during their own years of schooling with notions that the rich and famous are the makers of history, have rarely understood the importance and power of organized grass-roots movements in changing society. The power of the grass-roots movement should be an important theme woven through all school curricula.

Although a small group of individuals won the initial victory that established Fratney, it was a decision by the school board to hire more enlightened superintendents that allowed us to shift our focus from battling central office to dealing with more central educational issues.

These superintendents not only supported reform, but recognized that it can be achieved only by fostering grass-roots involvement.

School reform needs small groups of committed individuals at both the district leadership levels and the building and community levels. If only the former exists, school reform fails because it has a top-down, authoritarian style that alienates the teachers who must ultimately embrace the changes that need to take place in the classroom. If support from district leadership is lacking, however, the obstacles to reform are usually so great that grass-roots activists are consumed by senseless battles diverting attention from what really needs to be done.

Lesson 2: Multiracial unity is essential to successful school reform.

Another lesson from our experience is that multiracial unity is needed to move school reform forward. The initial organizing effort would have failed if African Americans, Latinos, and whites hadn't worked closely together. Working in multiracial groups in a racially divided society is difficult, however; the success of such efforts often depends on the underlying politics of the project and the individuals involved.

In considering issues of equality and multiculturalism, people must address the issues of power and voice straight on. Who is actually in control? Whose voice is actually being heard? At Fratney, we began by deciding that antiracism and the equality of all people would be values that are taught at all grade levels. Some people of color saw this action as a clear indication that the project was serious about building multiracial unity. We also set up decision-making groups that make parents and teachers partners in running the school. Finally, we tried to institutionalize power relationships between language-majority and language-minority students by making the two languages in question as equal as possible.

Lesson 3: Build in time to reflect and learn.

A successful school program usually can't be planned on the fly. Educators and parents must be willing and able to devote sufficient time to planning the program and, later, to assessing progress and governing the school. We were able to gain additional time for teachers by (1) shifting the afternoon recess to follow lunch recess, thus extending the lunchtime planning period; (2) arranging art, music, and physical education classes so teams of teachers have time together; and (3) starting school 10 minutes earlier, so that once a month children leave early and the staff have a half day for planning.

While finding time for staff to plan is difficult, getting time for parents and teachers to work together is even more problematic. We have found no easy solution, but have managed by making sure that our site-based council meetings are held regularly and run efficiently, so that maximum benefits come from them.

As the school has grown, the issue of time has emerged as a key problem: time to train new staff, to plan new curriculum, to develop and implement better forms of assessment, to learn from one another. If school districts expect new and veteran teachers to improve their practices and cope with increasingly difficult social situations, qualitatively more time for collaborative planning, staff development, and reflection will need to be structured into the school day and school year.

Lesson 4: Genuine parent involvement is critical.

Parent involvement needs to be substantive and far-reaching. It must extend beyond pizza fund-raisers and volunteering for field trips. The central issues are power, presence, and resources. Do parents exert real power during their time spent in the school? Do parents have an ongoing, daily presence in the school and the classrooms? Are the resources allocated to schools sufficient to organize parent involvement? The Fratney experience shows that parents are more likely to come to the school if they are able to exercise genuine power in decisions that directly affect the future of the school and their children's lives. At Fratney, this has meant having parents and teachers deal with issues such as curriculum, budget, facility renovation, and personnel (Peterson 1993).

Empowering parents may at times seem to work against the principles of a democratic school because some parents' ideas are neither progressive nor democratic. Parents across the United States, for instance, have supported book banning, lobbied for school prayer, and opposed equality and desegregation, the teaching of evolution, and multiculturalism (Karp 1993).

How does a school deal with this contradiction between the need to empower parents and at the same time promote progressive educational and social policies? First, structures must be created to engender ongoing debate and constant dialogue, and these structures must not privilege those people with college education or more free time. Discussion must not shy away from frank assessments of the program's goals, expected results, and alternative strategies for reaching the goals if recommended practices prove insufficient. Second, a group of people within the school must take on the task of promoting progressive policies and challenging others on such issues.

Lesson 5: Structures that foster change must be institutionalized.

Although the renaissance of any particular school must be defended, we must acknowledge the limitations of school-by-school reform. Most of the fine alternative schools of the 1960s died as their originators moved on. The success of many of these schools, Fratney included, is a result of many people spending enormous amounts of time and energy in a fight against the status quo. These kinds of efforts don't readily transfer from school to school. We must institutionalize structures that allow and foster change in the public schools and in the teaching profession. For instance, paid parent organizers, based at the school level, would substantively strengthen parent involvement. Assessment procedures that are not dependent on standardized achievement tests should be adopted at district, state, and national levels (i.e., for Chapter I programming) to push teachers toward more holistic assessment measures. Changes in state regulations governing the school calendar and hours should be made more flexible so schools can provide more time for collaboration and planning. Districtwide programs to support new and struggling veteran teachers should be created so that individual schools aren't forced to spend inordinate amounts of time or resources on such programs.

Lesson 6: Successful school reform is part of larger societal change efforts.

On a small scale, we have seen some success with the Fratney project. Parents, staff, and students continue to work together, albeit with occasional disagreement, to build a more humane, democratic school within our troubled society. The Fratney experience has shown us that the reform of any particular school must take place within a larger context of districtwide curricular reform and structural change. And the improvement of schools generally must be linked to changes in society. Large class sizes, lack of teacher planning time, and the broader problems of poverty, child abuse, and unemployment all reflect the triumph of private profit over human need.

How can a school community work in the context of the broader struggles to make a city, state, or nation a safer, healthier place to live? Our successful organizing campaign to rebuild our school tot lot was a small example of a how a neighborhood coalition can obtain funds for a project that benefits both the school and the neighborhood. Small efforts like this can be the foundations for the development of communitywide coalitions and projects to link the generic parent at a generic school to activities and movements that will improve schools and communities alike.

Ultimately, the success of Fratney and other similar school projects is bound up tightly to our efforts to achieve justice and equality in our society as a whole. For our efforts to bear fruit, we must have both a local vision and a national vision. Just as the consciousness of my 5th grade students was in many ways linked to the march on Washington for gay and lesbian rights, so too is the future of schools like Fratney linked to broader social movements. Our schools, our cities, our children will not survive the rising tide of poverty, inequality, and violence without a social movement that demands from the whole society what many are demanding from schools alone.

References

Ahlgren, P. (Fall 1993). "La Escuela Fratney: Reflections on a Bilingual, Anti-bias, Multicultural, Elementary School." *Teaching Tolerance* 2, 2: 26–31.

Banks, J. (1991). *Teaching Strategies for Ethnic Studies.* Boston: Allyn and Bacon.

Bowditch, C. (Winter 1993). "Responses to Michelle Fine's [Ap]parent Involvement: Reflections on Parents, Power, and Urban Public Schools." *Teachers College Record* 95, 2: 177–181.

Edelsky, C. (1991). "Not Acquiring Spanish as a Second Language: The Politics of Second Language Acquisition." In *With Literacy and Justice For All: Rethinking The Social in Language and Education.* New York: Falmer Press.

Karp, S. (1993). "Trouble Over the Rainbow." *Rethinking Schools* 7, 3: 8–10.

Levine, D. (1991). "A New Path to Learning." *Rethinking Schools* 6, 1: 1, 21, 23.

Miner, B. (1991). "Taking Multicultural/Anti-Racist Education Seriously: An Interview with Enid Lee." *Rethinking Schools* 6, 1: 6.

Peterson, R. (1987). "NCTE Issues Basal Report Card." *Rethinking Schools* 2, 3: 6–7.

Peterson, R. (1988). "Basal Adoption Controversy Continues into Second Year: Whole Language Pilot Projects Launched." *Rethinking Schools* 3, 1: 9.

Peterson, R. (1989). "Don't Mourn, Organize: Teachers Take the Offensive Against Basals." *Theory into Practice* 28, 4: 295–299.

Peterson, R. (1993). "Creating a School That Honors the Traditions of a Culturally Diverse Student Body: La Escuela Fratney." In *Public Schools That Work: Creating Community,* edited by Gregory A. Smith. New York: Routledge.

Tenorio, R. (1986). "Surviving Scott Foresman: Confessions of a Kindergarten Teacher." *Rethinking Schools* 1, 1: 1, 8.

Tenorio, R. (1988). "Recipe for Teaching Reading: Hold the Basal." *Rethinking Schools* 2, 3: 4.

5

The Situation Made Us Special

BARBARA L. BRODHAGEN

We Sign Our Constitution

The 7th grade classroom was alive with excitement and anticipation, students stretching their necks to try to look out the doorway. "Here he comes," somebody said. Students quickly composed themselves, and all eyes were on the principal as he entered the room. Acting as spokesperson for the class, one student said, "Mr. Principal, you have been asked here today to witness the reading and signing of our classroom constitution." One voice began as 55 others joined in:

> *We, the class of Rooms 201/202 at Marquette Middle School, in order to form the best class possible, pledge to live by the following statements:*

- *We appreciate our individual differences. We recognize that each person is unique.*
- *All individuals will be treated with respect and dignity. There is no room for put-downs in our room.*
- *We will be honest with one another in order to build trust.*
- *We will learn to resolve conflicts, which may involve learning to live with nonresolution.*
- *Each person will truly listen to every other person.*
- *We will cooperate and collaborate with one another.*
- *Learning will be meaningful.*
- *We recognize that people learn in different ways.*

- *Assignments, field trips, hands-on experiences will be varied so that everyone can and will learn. If everyone tries, we ALL will succeed.*
- *Having fun will naturally become part of our experiences.*
- *All individuals will be organized and on time.*
- *We will respect the right to pass (not take a turn).*

We agree to abide by these truths to the best of our abilities, both as unique individuals and as a cooperative and collaborative community.

One young person began to clap, and soon there were cheers and more applause for all of us, and each of us, and what we had done. The principal said some appropriate and encouraging words and left. We were a group of people, young adolescents and adults, who had just publicly stated agreement to all that was in our constitution, and each of us would try to honor its content to the best of our ability.

Few teachers would be willing to step into a classroom and attempt to engage more than four dozen 12- and 13-year-olds in meaningful discussion. We've all read about how unruly large groups of young adolescents can be, and many of us are afraid we would be unable to "keep control" in this setting. But if creating a democratic community is our goal, then every young person must have a chance to be heard, and teachers must be willing to listen. Achieving such a community is what this chapter is about. It is the story of how teachers and students at Marquette Middle School (now known as Georgia O'Keefe Middle School) in Madison, Wisconsin, worked together to create a democratic classroom.

Marquette Middle School has a culturally diverse enrollment of about 600 students, many of whom are eligible for free or reduced-price lunches. Classes are heterogeneously grouped, and students labeled as needing special education are integrated into all classes. School administrators have supported new teaching innovations.

During the two years from which this story is told, as many as 56 heterogeneously grouped students were assigned to two teachers who had responsibility for math/science and language arts/social studies. They were joined by a special education teacher who had been assigned to work with students labeled "learning disabled." Each semester, a student teacher from the university worked with us as well.

What Brought Me To This

I have been teaching for a long time. For many years, I worked with children identified as having a learning disability. This work gave me the unique opportunity to get into many classrooms in several school districts in Wisconsin and New York. Rarely did I see students in any of those classrooms participate in determining what they were to learn or how they would learn it.

A lot of what happened in those classrooms didn't seem to make sense to students, and teachers rarely tried to connect what students were learning from one class to the next. Students' usual routine was to sit and listen for 45 minutes and then go to the next class and do the same. When young people asked, "Why do we have to learn this?" or "Is this going to be on the test?" or "Do we have to remember this?" I was sometimes not really sure how to answer them. The students, both learning-disabled and not, were frustrated, and so was I.

As a result of these less-than-satisfying experiences as a teacher (as well as some during my own student years), I began talking to colleagues and friends, trying to create another view of school. We talked of designing school experiences that involve students in all aspects of classroom life, including curriculum planning. Curriculum integration, an idea I had almost forgotten, seemed to provide the theoretical framework needed for this endeavor. I recalled my teaching experiences in a self-contained, integrated middle school classroom for the learning-disabled. In that classroom, students planned their learning with me. They taught their hobbies and interests to one another. Those times had slipped away from me.

Integrative curriculum, planning with students, cooperative learning, team teaching—all were part of what I knew would help bring about successful teaching and learning experiences for teachers and students, including students labeled learning-disabled. I explained to our building administrators what I wanted to do, then set out to find someone who would team with me. Mary Ploeser, a math and science teacher, happily accepted my invitation. I was excited to start the school year.

We Create a Community

Teachers did not walk into the classroom on the first day of school and ask students to write a classroom constitution. We and our students were strangers, representing different neighborhoods, socioeconomic levels, and ethnic backgrounds. The first two days of the school year were filled with the busy work common to most schools: locker assignments, class schedules, school forms, and so on. We had, however, planned some introductory activities. Halfway through the second day, we asked students how they thought all of us might get to know one another and create a real community. This simple question was the first of many invitations for young people to help create a democratic community. Students did not hesitate; ideas poured forth.

The theme for the first two weeks was "Who are we? Who am I?" (a theme selected by the teachers). Students and teachers together decided that a survey to which everyone contributed questions would help us find out more about one another.

The group wanted to know where everyone had come from, so we designed a family history form, and each person went home and recorded all the countries their ancestors had come from. The information from the forms was used to make maps identifying these countries and to compute each country's distance from Madison. Students investigated whether the countries' names had changed by comparing old world maps to new world maps. These young adolescents, each trying to find his or her own identity, wanted to know what their names meant, so off they went to the library to research both first and last names. Teachers did these same activities. After all, we were members of the group too.

To help answer the question "Who am I?" we measured heights, gathered family health and education histories, wrote brief autobiographies (complete with snapshots), and compared individual data to the results of the class survey. We all marked the location of our homes on a local map. Students interviewed one another and made introductions to the entire group.

Students suggested there be rules for the class, both for teachers and for students. If there were to be rules, then those who would have to live by the rules needed to have a say. The group discussed whether these "things" should be called rules, guidelines, or a contract. One student suggested we write a constitution. Teachers led a review on constitutions, and students and teachers made separate lists of ideas that might be included in a class constitution. Both lists were displayed, and teachers and students debated and negotiated whether various requests were legitimate and, if they were, whether they belonged in our constitution. Teachers and students alike had to stand up and explain, provide evidence, or otherwise convince the group why a particular idea or statement was necessary. After reaching consensus, a committee of students and one teacher took the phrases, ideas, and sentences and fashioned them into the constitution quoted at the beginning of this chapter.

The constitution guided us throughout the school year. On numerous occasions, students, more than teachers, called the group's attention to statements made and agreed upon. They did not take the group's efforts lightly.

Other activities helped build community throughout the year. All of us participated in cooperative games, went to the school forest ropes course, had a potluck dinner, invited parents to see projects and hear presentations, shared our successes with other classes, and invited support staff to be part of the activities.

Another idea that initially met with snickers, but ended up being a favorite, was Monday morning "Sharing Time." Any student or students could share something they had done, something that had happened, or something they had heard about. On most Mondays, a time limit was necessary because so many students wanted to participate. We heard about many wonderful experiences and about the many stresses some young people lived under. Sharing Time gave all of us a chance to get to know different sides of people, what they did in their free time, what their family was like, and what they heard on the news. We valued this time and considered it an important part of our democratic community.

From this partial description of the first two weeks of school, you can see that students already had many opportunities to participate in the creation of a community. We listened to all ideas, and by doing so, honored the diversity represented in the classroom: female and male, rich and poor, adult and young adolescent, and people of many ethnic groups.

Our survey had shown us that we didn't agree on everything, but had decided that certain things were important to us all. We shared a sense of who we were, and we had begun to trust one another. We were becoming a community.

We Plan Together

The constitution written jointly by teachers and students stated that "learning will be meaningful." One way we try to assure meaningful learning is to involve students in planning the curriculum.

The purpose of our curriculum is to help young people extend their understanding of themselves and their world. Using a constructivist approach, we ask students to identify questions and concerns they have about self and the world.

Here are some of students' questions about self:

- How did my skin color come about?
- What will happen to me after I die?
- Why was I born who I am and into my family?
- Will my kids follow in my footsteps?
- Why is school so hard for me?
- How do my bodily organs keep going and going?
- How will I know if I am really in love?
- Will I be successful and happy?
- Why am I so short?

And here are some of students' questions about the world:

- Why do some people/groups think they are better?
- How did racism ever start?
- How did religions evolve?
- Is it possible for people to be born with both sex parts?
- Why are some people gay?
- When will gang violence ever stop?
- Why are so many politicians dishonest?
- Will there ever be a President who is not a white man?
- Will there ever be enough for all to survive?
- What would happen if the sun died?
- How was the universe created?
- How can birds fly?
- Will other planets be livable?
- Will the earth become so crowded that some will be sent to space?
- What will people evolve to look like in 100 years?
- Will there ever be a cure for AIDS?
- Why can't teenagers vote?
- How do roller coasters work?
- Why are some kids popular?
- Why do we only hear about the bad stuff?

Students first develop their questions individually and then work in small groups to try to find common or shared questions. Once the whole class has identified these questions, students are asked to find connections between the self and world questions. These connections form themes around which the curriculum is organized. Students have developed such themes as Isms; Outer Space; Time: Past and Present; Mind Bogglers; Environment; Death, War, and Violence; and Conflict.

As students consider each theme, they identify activities that respond to the self and world questions included in the theme. A curriculum containing activities suggested by students begins to accommodate individual learning styles, what a person likes to do or is good at. Students know that they need to develop a variety of skills, however. When asked what should happen if the only suggested activity was "to read," students were quick to respond that there has to be a balance; everyone needs to do the basics, "like reading, writing, and math, and all that other stuff we learn in school."

The teacher's role in this process is not the traditional one of always directing the action from the front of the classroom, but rather one of facilitating activities and collaborating with students. We help groups of students hold discussions, model how to ask clarifying questions, suggest ways to phrase questions, listen to be sure that one or two students don't control a group, and offer encouragement and suggestions. We help students hear others' ideas and periodically remind them that each person has a right to an opinion.

Many wonderful things can happen when students and teachers jointly plan the curriculum. Everyone has opportunities to participate in making decisions about what our work will be. Young people see their teachers listening to them and treating them seriously. Respect and trust between students and teachers grow as both observe how actions and words bring the curriculum to life. Early group planning creates a climate of openness for the rest of the year, a large part of which is a curriculum with far fewer "hidden" aspects than a traditional curriculum.

We Have Big Questions and Concerns

It would take many pages to list all the questions students have raised in our classroom. The self and world questions mentioned earlier should be enough to convince anyone that young people have limitless questions and concerns about themselves and the world. They are curious about almost everything and are trying hard to make sense of life in all its complexities, and to find out who they are and what they want to become. Their serious and thoughtful questions reflect a need to see themselves as members of a variety of groups within numerous cultures, including the dominant culture.

In the search to find answers, the group often went in directions not planned. One question usually led to several new questions, usually along the lines of *Why does it have to be that way?* or *Who says so?* or *Who makes the decisions?* or *Why don't we just change it?* Because democracy, dignity, and diversity were at the center of our classroom, we tried to look at each question and theme through these lenses. If students did not bring up these questions, teachers did. We wanted students to become accustomed to looking at what they studied with a critical eye and to considering as many different viewpoints as possible. For example, an activity in the "Isms" unit was designed to answer several questions about the relative anonymity of women who have invented things or spearheaded important social movements. Students studied women who have made notable contributions toward the improvement of humankind and then tried to locate information about these women in a huge stack of the school's social studies and history textbooks. Students were surprised to find little mention of the women in the textbooks and immediately wanted to know why they had been left out of these chronicles of history.

We talked about who writes textbooks, who owns textbook companies, how society has treated the contributions of women throughout history, and what people could do to hear the complete story. Students were reminded of other work done during the year that also highlighted the prevalent practice of omitting specific groups of people. Students learned that they can use textbooks to answer some questions, but they also learned that they need to consult a variety of sources for complete answers to some questions. Their research experiences showed them that there are sometimes discrepancies in the information presented in resources on the same topic, that "reliable" sources are not always accurate.

Anyone who has worked in a middle school can tell you that adolescents are concerned about fairness and justice in solving the problems of society. They are thinking through their own ideas about morality and going through the sometimes painful process of deciding whether they will continue to abide by the values "given" to them. We challenged students to think critically about their questions and encouraged them to keep asking tough questions of their teachers, their parents, and even their peers. The depth of young adolescents' questions is surprising even to teachers who work with them every day. We sometimes wonder whether we thought about these "big" questions when we were their age; we know that nobody ever encouraged us to.

When we asked parents to identify their own questions and concerns about themselves and the world as part of an "Open House" presentation, they came up with many of the same questions their children did:

- Where are the dirtiest and cleanest cities? cultures?
- Why aren't there more recycled products?
- Why do we kill so many animals for food?
- How can we create and save jobs and save the animals and the environment?
- What's the status of the space station?
- How much do we spend on outer space?
- Who owns outer space?
- Will racism ever stop?
- Why do people kill each other (not in war)?
- Will there ever be a time when everyone has enough to survive?
- What job will I have? What kind of jobs will there be?
- Will we keep growing in number until we're wiped out?
- Will kids ever be able to vote?

We believe students have the right to try to figure out how things got to be the way they are. There have been times, however, when we've stared at the long lists of questions and activities suggested by students and wondered how we would ever find the strength to teach about some of these overwhelming, real-life issues. During those moments, we remind ourselves of students' intense desire *to know why things are,* and then reaffirm our commitment to helping these kids find the answers.

I know that what happened in our classroom is not common. In many classrooms, questions from students are unwelcome. But we continue to believe that young people have the right to ask questions and the right to know. They have the right to be part of a school that deals with their questions seriously.

Students Are Involved in
Developing Their Own Evaluations

"Welcome to the Room 201/202 Museum."

"The museum tour is about to begin. Would you please line up behind your tour guide?" Groups of young people shuffle around, some find seats, others gather papers, and a small group lines up in the front of the room.

"My name is Lisa and I will be your first guide. I will explain to you what a rain forest is and where rain forests are located. Other guides will show and tell you about the products, climate, rainfall, groundwater, soil conditions, and endangered plants and animals of rain forests. You will also hear about indigenous peoples and reasons why the rain forests are in the news. And you will find out some strange but true facts about rain forests."

Looking around the room, visitors see more than a rain forest. A child's plastic swimming pool has been turned into a pond complete with water, grass, tadpoles, and a frog. There is a woodland forest made of branches covered with a variety of leaves and all sorts of stuffed animals: deer, raccoon, birds, and bear. A papier-mache snake slithers in desert sand as a vulture flies overhead. Visitors see groundwater displays, charts, posters, dioramas, and "Do you know?" displays. The room is alive with color.

At various points in the museum, student tour guides discuss different topics. At the front of the room, Jeff is describing the rain forest food chain. He holds up pictures of a poisonous tree frog and a leaf on which there are tiny insects. Then he replaces the picture of the frog with a picture of a toucan and begins to talk about animals and plants on the endangered species list.

At the close of the tour, the rain forest guides ask for questions. Many hands shoot into the air. The guides answer those questions they can and write down those they can't, assuring the group that the museum staff will "get right on it" and find the answers. They thank the group for coming and return to their seats as the next biome's guides move into place.

A lot had to happen before museum tours like this could take place. First, students had to decide what biome they wanted to study. Then the large group, including the teachers, had to determine the requirements to be met by each small group. Group members had to decide who was going to do what research. Research had to be completed before any construction could begin. Decisions had to be made about where biomes would be built. Maps needed to be drawn, reports written, speeches practiced, and on and on. The guided museum tour was each group's final evaluation for the "Environment" unit. The tour was videotaped by a teacher, the list of requirements checked by the teachers, and the tour evaluated by students.

Students often were involved in creating unit or theme evaluations, which might be a final group project, a presentation, or a written self-evaluation. For instance, students developed a multimedia presentation to teach a different age group about an "ism"; made a collage, book, or box to show what they thought life would be like in the future; completed individual and group requirements for a presentation about a planet in our solar system; and did community service as a part of the "Environment" unit. Teachers were willing to listen and negotiate with students when they presented their ideas about how evaluation might occur, sending students the message that their ideas mattered.

Students completed self-evaluations at the end of themes and marking periods. Teachers and students spent time discussing areas that the evaluation might include, such as quality and quantity of work, what was easy and hard, students' effort and interest, what they liked to do best or least, group versus individual work skills, and so on. After reviewing their "portfolio" of completed work, students wrote about what they thought they had learned. Finally, students wrote goals for the next marking period.

We Can't Believe How Much We've Learned

Every "product" or paper copy of each student's work was collected and kept to provide students a visible record of their work. This "portfolio" served as the basis for students' written self-evaluations. As students went through their papers, we heard time and time again, "I can't believe we did so much work."

Every student had a notebook to use as a processing journal. Near the end of each day, teachers put questions on the board that called for students to reflect on critical learnings or "big" concepts. The written responses to these questions allowed teachers to check in with every student and get feedback about our teaching. When many students could not answer the questions, we knew we had to provide additional learning experiences.

Teachers met with groups of eight to ten students to discuss the current theme and to consider students' concerns, reactions to activities, or requests for additional teaching or practice. Teachers used this time to bring up critical learnings that students should be mastering, to ask students to explain what they have been doing, and to ask for feedback about a variety of things.

At the end of each theme, teachers and students attempted to list the knowledge and skills students had needed to answer their questions. We realized that this new curriculum approach would prompt someone to ask for documentation of students' learning. What better way for us to gather this information than by asking the group? By middle school, most students are able to use the language of education, so they listed, for example, "read, write, communicate, do research, use math, work with maps, graphs, and tables, use the scientific method, use computers, listen, give reports, and work in groups."

Listing learnings on the board, talking in small processing groups, and having individuals write in a processing journal all helped us know whether students were learning. At times, the group was amazed at how much they had accomplished and learned. By answering their own questions, the young people could see a purpose in learning, for example, how to compute the mean, median, and mode, or how to contact an environmental agency. They had many opportunities to see the connection between the what, how, and why of learning because they were being asked to create knowledge based on their own real work; they were being asked to actively educate themselves.

We wanted students to learn a lot—and to know that they had. We wanted them to be able to reflect on the most recent theme or the entire year and clearly see their many accomplishments. We wanted them to understand that even though they were not studying the separate subjects of the traditional curriculum, they were learning much of what the "education community" said they should learn.

Everyone Works Together

Students worked with one another much of the time. Often we had each student name one person with whom she or he felt able to work; then teachers structured heterogeneous cooperative learning groups. The groups stayed constant throughout an activity and sometimes throughout an entire theme. We tried to change the make-up of groups across the year, however, so that students had opportunities to work with all of their classmates. The strategy must have worked, because our students have told us that in other classes they knew only a few of their classmates, but in our classroom they know everyone.

Our constitution called for collaboration and cooperation. We wanted to eliminate as much competition as possible. The students who had the most difficulty adjusting to a lack of obvious competition were the high-achieving students. Because they were not completing lots of worksheets or individual assignments, but instead were doing individual and group projects, they initially were unsure they were still doing well. After several weeks, however, these students began to see that cooperating with others did not compromise their own academic work. They also realized that the projects and other activities in our curriculum were more challenging and sophisticated than the worksheets they were used to completing.

Students began to see that they could be teachers to each other and did not depend as much on the "official" teachers. After all, the teachers were often trying to answer questions along with the students. By learning together, we were experiencing the creation of knowledge based on our questions. We worked together toward a common goal important to us all, and when a unit was finished, we applauded and cheered in celebration of all completed projects and presentations.

Do You Want to Talk to Our Class?

We frequently invited people from the community to our class to help us try to answer the questions students had raised. Students were always suggesting, "Bring in an expert." It was astounding how many human resources students helped us locate. They knew all sorts of people, and those we called were glad to help out, especially if we mentioned the name of the student who had made the recommendation. Our presenters were usually surprised at how specific our requests for information were, and many commented on how well prepared the class was for their visit. Some were also surprised at the topics being studied.

We wanted to open students' minds to many career possibilities, so our presenters were almost always asked to talk about the education needed for their present occupation. White-collar professionals, tradespeople, service providers, retired workers, people working in jobs out of the mainstream, and even an AIDS care provider came to speak to us. Our class learned from these people, and they learned from us.

Students Join the Parent-Teacher Conferences

Everything was set. All the student work portfolios were in order, the room was relatively pleasant, the table and chairs were in position, and I was nervous. "Will this really work?" I wondered. "Will these kids really conduct their own parent-student-teacher conferences? Had there been enough preparation? Will parents want to listen to their child?"

I glanced at the clock and knew it was time. My first conference was with Holly, a bright young adolescent who does consistently good work, but doesn't seem to want to participate in large- or small-group discussions.

Holly walked into the room first and came right to the table and sat down. Trailing behind was her mother, who was carrying a younger sibling. I slid Holly's folder toward her, waiting for her to make introductions. "And who is this?" I asked, as I leaned over and touched the sibling's hand. With that, Holly began.

She introduced her mother, her sister, and me and then plunged into discussion of her work. "This is my best work." She took papers out and gave a brief explanation of each. Her mom asked questions and made comments such as "I remember when you were working on this" and "This turned out pretty good." Holly explained that the "best work" papers would be kept at school in a folder that would be sent home at year's end, with all the other best work.

Holly then read her written self-evaluation to her mom. When she had finished, she and her mom started to talk about why Holly didn't want to talk in front of her peers. Her mom admitted that as a teenager she didn't want to talk in class either. They talked about what was easy and challenging for Holly. They laughed about Holly's admission that doing her homework in front of the television wasn't such a good idea. And they discussed her goals for the next quarter, with mom saying Holly was too hard on herself.

I just sat there, amazed. Holly had said all I would have said, and much more that I never could or should. I simply validated a lot of what they had said. When it was over, the three of us stood, smiling at one another, exchanging looks that seemed to say, "This felt good, let's do it again."

The parent-teacher conferences held in previous years were always somewhat disappointing for us. Students, the critical focus of the conference, usually were not even present. We decided to begin our overhaul of the conferences by asking students how they thought the conferences should be structured. They were quick to point out that the parents or other concerned adults who attended these conferences heard the same things year after year: "Dan could do better if he only would pay attention." "Brian should participate more in class." "Jamie is doing just fine." "Ali doesn't complete her assignments." "Tim talks with his friends too much during class." Students said their parents would come home from the conference and ground them if they had done poorly or hardly talk about the conference at all if it had gone well. They asked if it wouldn't be more beneficial to talk about their good points, since both the student and parent generally already knew what the student should do better.

Together we decided that conferences would focus on what students defined as their best work and also include a review of students' written self-evaluations and goals. "Best work" was a collection of five or six pieces students selected using their own criteria. These might have included a favorite, one that received a good grade, one that was of interest, or one that looked hard; some students chose papers that represented a cross-section of work in writing, math, social studies, or other areas. The remainder of students' work was available for review and would be sent home at the conclusion of the conference.

As you can see from Holly's conference, what really sets these conferences apart is that students direct the action, from making necessary introductions and beginning the conference to wrapping up the discussion at the appropriate time. Students can begin the conference with a discussion of any of the three sections of the conference folder: (1) the written self-evaluation, (2) the official school report card, or (3) the best work. At some point in the discussion, however, they must describe what they have been studying and show the related work, highlighting their best work. During most conferences, parents ask clarifying questions that prompt students to offer additional information. The written self-evaluation can be read aloud by the student or given to the parent to read. Goals, too, must be discussed.

The teacher enters into the conversation only as needed. We've found that students are quite capable of assessing their strengths and weaknesses; in many cases, we've even had to soften their too-harsh self-evaluations.

For many of these young people and their parents, the conferences are one of the few times they actually discuss the work of the student. Most students can point out what they are good at and what they still need to work on. All the discussion points from the old conference format come out through the self-evaluation and goals discussion, but this new conference format gives students a large measure of control over what and how things are said. Shifting who has the "power" in various situations is an important part of creating a democratic classroom.

We Look Back on Our Experiences

It is now two years since I began working with and in an integrative curriculum where student-teacher planning is a given. I can no longer imagine not involving the learners, no matter their age, in planning their education and running "our" classroom. Each school year, students have clearly demonstrated that they are able and willing to actively participate in planning and designing their own education.

Some students initially said the work of planning the curriculum was too difficult and asked, "Why don't you teachers just do all of it?" We were asking them to become learners who actively participate in all aspects of their education, from planning to evaluation, and most had never been asked to do anything like that before. They were uncomfortable with changing the role of students. The role of teachers changed too. Sometimes teachers were still disseminators of information, but more often we were learners as well as facilitators of learning.

Teachers and students struggled to define and act on these new roles. Deciding when students would participate in decisions and when teachers alone would make decisions was a recurring issue. Students sometimes challenged teachers to explain why students couldn't be part of all decisions. Many times, we had no answer for them. We were still trying to figure out how much power could or should be given to students. All of us were learning firsthand how difficult it can be to put democratic principles into action.

Student-teacher planning of the curriculum was a messy process. There wasn't a neat curriculum guide or textbook to turn to for lessons. Identifying the significant concepts that would tie a theme together took a lot of time, but without this identification, a theme could become a series of "sound bites" that did little to satisfy students' need to learn. And there were many times when teachers had to scramble to find appropriate materials and resources. Fortunately, we had the much-needed planning time to accomplish these tasks.

Colleagues' reactions to our efforts varied greatly. Some thought we were just going into class and doing whatever the students wanted to do. Some wondered if we were teaching anything. Some knew and understood what we were doing, but said they would never try it because they could see how much extra work it requires. Very few asked to talk with us about our work, yet we knew some were talking about it without us being present to explain. The administration didn't put up any roadblocks, but nobody made many overt efforts to invite others to critically consider the nature and substance of our work.

At the time I became involved in this effort, I didn't think about it as trying to create a democratic classroom. I wanted the students to work with teachers in creating an exciting, rich, and meaningful curriculum. I wanted to see and hear for myself that young people can learn and want to learn. I didn't know how the effort would turn out, and I still have many questions, but they concern implementation rather than theory. As I have said, I can't go back.

The teachers involved in this endeavor interviewed former students to learn what they miss the most about our classrooms. They miss having a say in what they learn, being able to study something in depth, working in groups, knowing they can bring up an issue even if it isn't on the agenda, making presentations about what they learned, talking politics, and participating in making decisions about much of the day-to-day life of the classroom.

As part of the interview, we asked the group if they thought the computer had perhaps generated a "special" group rather than the diverse, heterogeneous one it was directed to. After all, our time together had been such a great success in so many ways for nearly everyone involved that the experience seemed almost too good to be true. After some discussion, one student said what we all felt: " . . . We weren't a special group, but the situation made us special."

6

Lessons from Democratic Schools

MICHAEL W. APPLE AND JAMES A. BEANE

W e live in a time when the very meaning of democracy is being radically changed. Rather than referring to ways in which political and institutional life are shaped by equitable, active, widespread, and fully informed participation, democracy is increasingly being defined as un-regulated business maneuvers in a free market economy. Applied to schools, this redefinition has given rise to the push for tax credits and vouchers, management by private firms, commercialized media and materials, and abandonment of the broader ideals of public education (Apple 1993). This degradation has extended to the point where a private consulting firm has recommended that "public" be dropped from "public schools" because its similar use in conjunction with housing, libraries, radio, and assistance programs has come to have negative connotations. Such is the power of language manipulation: Social commitments for the common good are now made out to be "public nuisances."

The schools described in this book are part of a larger movement that eschews this redefinition of democracy in education. They are deeply involved in finding practical ways to increase the meaningful participation of everyone involved in the educational experience, including parents, local residents, and especially students themselves. From their experiences, we can see that this goal is attainable through the creation of learning communities within each school and between the school and the larger community (see also Smith 1993).

The curriculum in all of these schools is based on the belief that knowledge comes to life for students and teachers only when it is connected to something that is serious. Rigorous intellectual work is prized, not for the sake of symbolic standards or agreeable publicity, but because of its ability to make a difference in how we understand and act powerfully on the social world in which we live. The implications for a process of assessment dramatically different from the relatively mechanical and reductive standardized procedures used by so many school systems are visible in these pioneering schools as well.

The idea of a thematic curriculum dominates these schools, not simply as an effective methodology that keeps kids happy, but because this approach involves putting knowledge to use in relation to real-life problems and issues (Beane 1993). The focus on what is called "unmet community needs" in Rindge, on social and environmental issues at Fratney and Marquette, or on finding answers to "serious questions" at Central Park East is there because knowledge is thought about differently. Rather than being lists of concepts, facts, and skills that students master for standardized achievement tests (and then go on to forget, by and large), knowledge is that which is intimately connected to the communities and biographies of real people. Students learn that knowledge makes a difference in people's lives, including their own.

This view of knowledge can be seen in the emphasis at Rindge on transforming vocational education. Here, vocational education is not simply teaching future workers the flexible job skills supposedly needed for the 21st century, for despite political and educational rhetoric to the contrary, most economic forecasts show that a large proportion of the jobs the modern economy is creating are low-skilled, part-time, and poorly paid (Apple 1989). Vocational education at Rindge is designed as preparation for an enhanced model of active citizenship in which all people are empowered to make important decisions about the institutions in which they live and work—now and in the future. This same understanding can be seen in the emphasis at Marquette, Fratney, and Central Park East on developing curricula that speak to the present concerns and future dreams of the students, teachers, and communities that have so much to gain and lose in these schools.

We do not want to be dewy-eyed romantics here. The authors of these chapters are honest about the challenges they still face: financial cuts, pressure from powerful groups to define school purposes in terms of business community needs, ultraconservative attacks on programs and materials, the obsession with measuring anything that moves in the classroom, bureaucratic intransigence, and a society that has been told that public schools can't work in creative ways. What is perhaps most impressive about these schools is their remarkable progress in the face of such challenges. There are lessons to be learned here.

One fact that emerges clearly from these accounts is the attention educators give to the "mundane" realities of daily life in schools. These stories remind us that the most powerful meaning of democracy is formed not in glossy political rhetoric, but in the details of everyday lives. In these schools, people take seriously the realities of curriculum development, teaching, assessment, and the lives of students and teachers who must cooperate to make schools actually work. To say that people are committed to such matters may seem a needless restatement of the obvious; after all, the same topics are part of almost any "reform" talk in almost any faculty room. What is striking about these educators, however, is that they refused to allow the difficult financial stringencies, the often unwieldy bureaucratic regulations, and the immense social pressures and demands placed on schools to get in the way of building educational experiences that make a real difference in the lives of their students. In viewing such conditions as challenges to be dealt with, not excuses for inaction, these educators have shown a quality that more of us should aspire to, the quality of uncommon courage.

These educators have also managed to evoke an education that is both disciplined and caring; they do not provide formulas for students, teachers, or administrators. An education of this sort is the result of hard work by *everyone* involved. From our experience with the educators writing in this book, we know such work is compelling and fulfilling, but almost always exhausting. Yet, as almost any educator knows, we are all exhausted at the end of a day spent dealing with the realities of schools. The people whose voices you have heard here, however, have made a choice: Rather than spending most of their time on administrative tasks, curricula, teaching, and evaluation that are disconnected from their students and from the communities that they serve, rather than continuing to reproduce the conditions that make so many of our most talented teachers and administrators feel frustrated in their day-to-day lives, they have decided to make a break. They have decided to devote their lives as educators to engaging in educational activity organized around democratic social and pedagogic principles in which they strongly believe. In other words, they have chosen to be exhausted as a result of something worthwhile.

Our analysis to this point implies that these chapters, and their authors, describe an important break from "traditional" practice. Well, yes and no. They do stand as articulate statements about what is possible in schools if people are willing to move away from simply echoing the rhetoric of democracy and instead take up the practical tasks involved in building more democratic schools. As we note in Chapter 1, however, these schools and classrooms have not broken away from a tradition; they have found their way back to it. One of the distinct tragedies of today's school reform efforts is that the people involved have almost no knowledge of the long and valued tradition of like-minded efforts. Unfortunately, educators and citizens alike seem to have virtually no collective memory of the many successful attempts at building more democratic schools. The history of progressive school reform documents the fact that thousands of teachers, administrators, community activists, and others spent their entire professional lives trying to build more educationally and socially responsive institutions. We have much to gain by reconnecting with their successes and with how they approached and overcame difficulties. All progressively inclined educators stand on the shoulders of these people, people whose eloquent vision and hard work day in and day out stand as reminders that what the educators in this book are now doing in real schools is a continuation of a long and wide river of democracy. Our tasks as educators are to keep the river flowing on course and to enable all of the children of this nation to participate in this process.

We have presented four descriptions of democratic schools in this book. There are many, many more that could and probably should be shared among us. In our inner cities, in rural areas, and elsewhere, dedicated educators and community members have formed coalitions to take democracy seriously. One of the very real dilemmas educators face is finding out what is going on in school systems throughout this country where progressive schooling is making an impact. Part of the problem is simply time. Our work has become so intensified (Apple 1988, 1993) that not only is it difficult to find time to write about our successes, it is sometimes difficult to find time to even read about what other people are doing to transform their schools. Yet sharing our stories is crucial, as is teaching one another what can be done, what pitfalls to avoid, and what reality is like when the hard work of building more responsive schools finally pays off.

There are many places where educators can turn to tell their stories and to hear what others are doing: groups such as Rethinking Schools in Milwaukee, the Institute for Democracy in Education in Ohio, Educators for Social Responsibility, the National Coalition of Educational Activists, and publications such as *Teaching Tolerance, Rethinking Schools, Democracy and Education,* and *Equity and Excellence.* These groups and publications provide forums for sharing and hearing that will do much to counter the cynicism and despair that many educators feel when confronted with the daily difficulties of doing their jobs well in these uncertain times.

We include ourselves in the group that wants to learn about what is happening in the schools, because we understand that philosophical statements can find meaning only in the light of the experiences of real schools. We encourage you to tell us about your own experience in establishing programs similar to those described here. We may find, then, that this volume becomes only the first in a series recounting the rise of democratic schools. In this way, we can document that our best hope for countering the arrogant tendencies now being pushed on schools by groups with authoritarian political agendas, by the centralizers, and by the privatizers is to demonstrate that there are public schools that *do* work, and they do so by bringing real democracy to life. Our children's lives and futures are at stake. Let's not wait for others to act.

References

Apple, Michael W. (1988). *Teachers and Texts.* New York: Routledge.

Apple, Michael W. (1989). "American Realities: Poverty, Economy, and Education." In *Dropouts from School: Issues, Dilemmas, and Solutions,* edited by Lois Weis, Eleanor Farrar, and Hugh G. Petrie. Albany: State University of New York Press.

Apple, Michael W. (1993). *Official Knowledge: Democratic Education in a Conservative Age.* New York: Routledge.

Beane, James A. (1993). *A Middle School Curriculum.* Columbus, Ohio: National Middle School Association.

Smith, Gregory A. (1993). *Public Schools That Work.* New York: Routledge.

About the Authors

Michael W. Apple is John Bascom Professor of Curriculum and Instruction and Educational Policy Studies, University of Wisconsin, 225 N. Mills Street, Madison, WI 53706.

James A. Beane is Professor in the National College of Education, National-Louis University, Evanston, Illinois. Address correspondence to Dr. Beane at 928 West Shore Drive, Madison, WI 53715.

Barbara L. Brodhagen teaches for the Madison Metropolitan Public Schools in Madison, Wisconsin. She can be reached at 928 West Shore Drive, Madison, WI 53715.

Deborah Meier is a former Co-Director of Central Park East Secondary School in New York City. She is a Senior Fellow of the Annenberg Institute for School Reform and is President of the Center for Collaborative Education.

Bob Peterson teaches 5th grade at La Escuela Fratney in Milwaukee, Wisconsin. He is an editor of *Rethinking Schools,* which is available from Rethinking Schools, Ltd., 1001 E. Keefe Ave., Milwaukee, WI 53212. Phone: (414) 964-9646.

Larry Rosenstock is Executive Director of the Rindge School of Technical Arts, 459 Broadway, Cambridge, MA 02138, and is a Lecturer at the Harvard Graduate School of Education.

Paul Schwarz is Co-Director of Central Park East Secondary School, 1573 Madison Avenue, New York, NY 10029, and is a Thomson Fellow at the Coalition of Essential Schools.

Adria Steinberg is Academic Coordinator of the Rindge School of Technical Arts, 459 Broadway, Cambridge, MA 02138, and is a Lecturer at the Harvard Graduate School of Education.